ADVANCED SPORT FISHING
and
AQUATIC RESOURCES HANDBOOK

Authored by
Bob Schmidt

Edited by
Louis R. Jensen, Ed.D.

Associate Editor
Sharon Rushton

Graphics by
John Rice

Published through a grant from the American Sportfishing Association, formerly the American Fishing Tackle Manufacturers Association

The Future Fisherman Foundation is the educational arm of the American Sportfishing Association

American
Sportfishing Association

KENDALL/HUNT PUBLISHING COMPANY
4050 Westmark Drive   Dubuque, Iowa 52002

About the Author

Bob Schmidt is a freelance outdoor writer residing in Chicago. He was the first editor of *In-Fisherman Magazine* and then worked fourteen years as a writer and editor in educational publications for elementary school through junior college students. He has been a full-time freelance outdoor writer since 1982, writing three books and one booklet on fishing for the Boy Scouts of America, and contributing articles to outdoor magazines and writing for consumer and trade publications. He is a graduate of the Marquette University College of Journalism and past president of the Association of Great Lakes Outdoor Writers.

About the Graphic Artist

John Rice is a freelance illustrator residing in New York City. He is a frequent contributor to *Field & Stream* and his drawings appear in *McClaine's Game Fish of North America.* He had his first one-man show in 1985 and his artwork has been auctioned for Trout and Ducks Unlimited. He is a graduate of Visual and Performing Arts, Syracuse University.

Printed in the United States of America
10 9 8 7 6 5 4 3 2 1

TABLE OF CONTENTS

Preface   v

Acknowledgements   vii

SECTION A—FISHING—THE SPORT

Chapter 1—An Introduction to Fishing   1

Chapter 2—Fishing Safely   7

Chapter 3—Selecting, Matching, and Using Fishing Tackle   13

Chapter 4—Terminal Tackle, Line, Baits, Lures, and Accessories   23

Chapter 5—Locating Fish   33

Chapter 6—Fishing from Shore   39

Chapter 7—Fishing from Boats   45

Chapter 8—Caring for Your Catch   55

Chapter 9—Fishing Ethics and Your Personal Commitment   61

SECTION B—FISH—UNDERSTANDING THEIR BIOLOGY AND HABITAT TO BECOME A BETTER ANGLER

Chapter 10—Fish Biology   67

Chapter 11—Identification of Common Sport Fish   73

Chapter 12—Food Chains and Ecology   81

Chapter 13—Fish Behavior   89

SECTION C—WATER AND THE ENVIRONMENT

Chapter 14—Water as an Environment   99

Chapter 15—Aquatic Communities   105

Chapter 16—Effect of Human Culture on Aquatic Resources   111

Chapter 17—Managing Fish for Everyone   119

Appendix A—Fishing for a Career!   125

Appendix B—Glossary   129

PREFACE

AN IMPORTANT MESSAGE TO ALL PARENTS AND ADULTS

It is very important to give our children proper recreation that will not only entertain them for now but will enlighten them throughout their lives.

Today's world is full of distractions which take away from families being together and spending good quality time with each other. One of the biggest problems facing our children today is drug abuse. We, as parents and adults, must take an active interest in our children's behavior. We must provide the support and guidance which are needed to resist drugs. We are the role models for our children. Our life styles and attitudes will be copied by future generations. It is up to us to make the difference today and set the proper examples of right and wrong.

A great way to improve family communication is involvement in fishing. Fishing takes you away from the distractions of everyday life and puts you in touch with your children. There are no TVs or telephones to interfere while you are fishing. This quiet time creates the perfect environment for listening and talking.

You say you don't know how to fish or don't know much about fishing! Don't be ashamed to admit that to yourself or to your children. Learning together will help make you and your family a better group of anglers, and at the same time help your children to build self-esteem, self-confidence and self-respect. Taking time for fun can be a positive alternative to drugs.

Please join us in helping our youth enjoy a drug-free environment while enjoying fishing as a life-long form of recreation and entertainment.

ACKNOWLEDGEMENTS

Many people can take credit for the development of this *Advanced Sport Fishing and Aquatic Resources Handbook,* for it was truly a team effort. The initial step was taken by the Aquatic Resource Education Council who provided support for the development of aquatic resource education programs by developing the *Aquatic Resources Education Curriculum,* a manual for teachers, in 1987. Without this momentous preliminary step, support by the AFTMA Sport Fishing Education Foundation (now the American Sportfishing Association, ASA), the development of this student manual would not have happened.

Both the author, Bob Schmidt, and the graphic artist, John Rice, have produced outstanding work to ensure the highest quality student materials available for aquatic resources education.

The experience, support, and suggestions of aquatic education professionals from numerous states and the U.S. Fish and Wildlife Service had notable impact in shaping the content, scope, and sequence of this student manual. A thank you goes to the numerous organizations, businesses and individuals who provided input on specific areas. Special gratitude is extended to the following group of professionals who critically reviewed the entire text:

American Sportfishing Association—Norville Prosser

Connecticut Department of Environmental Protection, Bureau of Fisheries—George Babey

Georgia Department of Natural Resources—Spud Woodward

Iowa Department of Natural Resources—Barb Giger

Maryland Department of Natural Resources—Janet Hammed

Minnesota Division of Parks and Recreation—Judy Thomson

New Mexico Game and Fish Department—Dan Shaw and Don MacCarter

Ohio Division of Wildlife—James R. Wentz

Oregon Department of Fish and Wildlife—Bill Hastie

University of Oklahoma Department of Zoology—Dr. Loren G. Hill and Graduate Students

Washington Department of Wildlife—Michael O'Malley

U.S. Fish and Wildlife Service—Dave McDaniels

U.S. Fish and Wildlife Service, Region 1—Tammy Peterson

Two exceptional teachers, who both have received awards for their outstanding teaching, developed student activities which will be of interest to students of all ages:

Judy Elsey, Science Teacher, Sarah Scott Middle School—Terre Haute, Indiana

Ben Wernz, Science Department Chair, Woodrow Wilson Middle School, Terre Haute, Indiana

A special thanks is extended to Sharon Rushton, Executive Director of the Future Fisherman Foundation, for her untiring efforts in communicating with, between, and among the state aquatic education and association professionals and the editor. Her labors have greatly enhanced the quality of the text.

This *Advanced Sport Fishing and Aquatic Resources Handbook* was made possible through the American Sportfishing Association and its educational arm the Future Fisherman Foundation. The Association's leadership is to be commended for its farsightedness and concern for the long-term advancement of aquatic resources by sponsoring the development of aquatic resources educational programs.

Louis R. Jensen
Indiana State University

AN INTRODUCTION TO FISHING

THE HISTORY OF FISHING

Fishing is older than recorded history, and no one knows when prehistoric people first used tools or devices to catch fish. They probably caught fish in shallow water using their bare hands. Later, some may have built dams to divert small creeks or streams and then easily captured fish left stranded on the bottom. Archaeologists have discovered evidence that these people also used spears, traps, and nets for catching fish.

Stone Age anglers used some sort of line, probably vines. Instead of tying on hooks as we know them today, they used a "gorge." Gorges were made from bone, flint, thorns, turtle shell, or wood and tapered to a sharp point at each end. Some had grooves near the middle to attach a line. The gorge was inserted in bait. When a fish swallowed the bait-covered gorge and the line was drawn tight, it lodged in the fish's gullet or throat. Gorges have been discovered in many parts of the world.

Gorge

Primitive Hooks

The fish hook was invented about 7,000 years ago. Early hooks were made of copper. Later, fish hooks were made of bronze and iron, while today they are made of steel. Fishing poles and lines have been around for a long time, too. Chinese writing from about 4,000 years ago describes wooden fishing poles and lines made of silk. Fishing lines have been made of woven plant fibers, human hair, horsehair, cotton, and linen. Since the 1950's, nylon and other synthetic materials have been used.

Fishing rods have been made from many materials, including bamboo and steel. Today, most fishing rods are made of fiberglass or combinations of fiberglass, carbon graphite, and other space-age materials.

More than 300 years ago, the English were given credit for inventing the fishing reel. However, recent evidence suggests that the Chinese may have

been first. Paintings by 12th and 14th Century Chinese artists show anglers using fishing rods with reels. Early versions of modern reels were developed by watchmakers in Kentucky sometime between 1800 and 1810.

WHY AND HOW PEOPLE FISH

Throughout history people have fished to provide food for themselves, to catch and sell fish to other people, and for fun and sport.

Subsistence Fishing. Subsistence living is gathering (as opposed to growing) enough food for survival, and fishing was part of early peoples' basic method of survival. In parts of the world today, including the United States and especially in urban areas, many people continue to fish for subsistence reasons.

A variety of gear is used in subsistence fishing, including modern nets and traps. Gigs, spears with one or several barbed points, and harpoons are used for shallow-water subsistence fishing.

Commercial Fishing. Commercial fishing is different than subsistence fishing because the fish are caught and then sold to others. Commercial fishing provides fish and other seafood for people who can't or don't wish to catch these food items for themselves.

Commercial fishing is work—not a social or pleasure-time activity. The object is to earn a living.

This is not to say that commercial fishing isn't enjoyable, only that its main purpose is not enjoyment.

Commercial fishing usually requires a large sum of money for boats, nets, and other gear. It is a risky business because the amount of fish harvested and money earned depends on the weather, market prices, competition, and the availability of fish populations.

Sometimes "long lines" are used in commercial fishing to catch offshore species like swordfish, shark, and sailfish. Long lines may be several miles long and have a float at each end. Short lines, each with a lure or baited hook, are connected to this main line. A boat travels the line to collect the fish and re-bait the hooks.

Commercial fishing also uses nets to capture fish. Purse seine nets are used to enclose an area of water to catch fish, while gill nets are used to catch swimming fish.

Commercial fishing catches offshore fish such as halibut, swordfish, shark, and tuna. Deep-water species, such as cod, halibut, and sea bass, are taken by hook and line or with deep-water nets. Inshore species, including bluefish, flounder, perch, and shad, are taken by net. Saltwater commercial fishermen also supply consumers with shellfish such as crabs, lobsters, scallops, and shrimp.

Commercial fishing is also practiced in fresh water. Several freshwater species, including bloater chubs, whitefish, and yellow perch, are harvested in the Great Lakes. In smaller bodies of water, buffalo, carp, and catfish are caught for commercial purposes.

Fish for commercial sale can be obtained by fish farming. Fish farmers buy land, build ponds or waterways, and stock fish to raise and later sell. Fish farming is similar to cattle feeding where the animals are fed and sold for a profit. Popular species of fish produced by fish farms include catfish and rainbow trout.

Sport Fishing. Fishing for enjoyment is called sport fishing. Although the fish caught are often eaten, sport fishing isn't subsistence fishing. Sport fishing isn't commercial fishing either because the catch is not sold for a profit.

Handline

Sport fishing methods include everything from fishing with a simple handline to advanced methods such as offshore or Great Lakes trolling and fly fishing. Fly fishing, fishing only with artificial lures, trolling, surf casting, and fishing with light tackle are all popular.

Some anglers attempt to set International Game Fish Association (IGFA) records or compete in fishing tournaments. Others become involved with fishing-related hobbies, such as fly tying, lure making, rod building, and taxidermy.

THE SOCIAL AND ECONOMIC IMPACT OF FISHING

Commercial Fishing. Commercial fishing has a great impact on society. It provides food stores with fresh, frozen, dried, smoked, canned, and salted fish of many species. It benefits society by providing a variety of healthful and tasty food for the diet that otherwise would be unavailable for many people. Even sport anglers would normally be restricted to eating only a few local species if it were not for commercial fishing.

Commercial fishing provides jobs for boat owners, fishing boat captains and crews, fish farmers, canners, fish-processing plants, fishing gear manufacturers, shipping and trucking companies, food wholesalers, food stores, and restaurants. As with any industry, there's also a "ripple effect," which benefits other industries in some way. These beneficiaries include the food, housing, clothing, automotive, and gasoline industries. In many areas, entire coastal communities have been built around commercial fishing.

Sport Fishing. The total economic value of sport fishing is greater than commercial fishing. This is partly true because of the money spent by anglers for rods, reels, line, lures, hooks, bait, motors, boats, electronic instruments, launching and docking fees, and expenses for traveling to and staying at a fishing site (fuel, lodging, and food).

Sport fishing also has a ripple effect throughout a community. Anglers' dollars help the suppliers and manufacturers of other goods and services and provide jobs to many people. Because of these values to a community, many sponsor fishing tournaments or special angling events to attract people.

According to the National Survey of Fishing, Hunting and Wildlife Associated Recreation, anglers spend more that $24 billion annually pursuing their sport. In contrast, the approximate dockside value of commercial landings (fish catches) is $1.7 billion annually, with the equivalent retail value reaching $9.2 billion.

WHAT ANGLERS WANT

Sport fishing enthusiasts hold varying opinions and ideas about what constitutes quality fishing. Some people like to catch many fish and are not particularly concerned about size. Other people want to catch large fish. Some people want to catch fish to eat and other anglers release every fish they catch.

The job of fishery managers is to provide a sustained supply of a variety of fishing opportunities

for the sport fishing public. Whenever possible, the goal is to give the public a proper and effective balance. In addition to maintaining appropriate habitat for the fish, fishery managers can affect the quality and quantity of fish populations with regulations such as daily, possession, size, and slot limits.

BECOMING AN ANGLER

It's important to remember that fishing provides different things to different people. Fishing offers great enjoyment in many ways. Fishing lets some people get away from the hustle and bustle of the daily routine to enjoy our nation's rich natural resources. Some see fishing as an exciting and demanding sport. Others enjoy friendly competition with other anglers.

Whatever your reason for fishing, you need to know more than how to use a rod and reel if you are to become a successful and ethical angler. Learning about aquatic resources—the things living in or on the water and the habitat that supports them—is important. That's why this manual is called *Sport Fishing and Aquatic Resources*.

With this manual, you will gain greater appreciation for our most important aquatic resource—water. You will learn where fish live—aquatic habitat. You will be introduced to a variety of fish and habitats. You will learn that how you treat the resources in your state can impact fishing in another state or in several states. In your lifetime, you will hopefully have an opportunity to travel to other parts of the country. This book will help you become familiar with fishing techniques for species that may not exist in your home state.

ACTIVITIES

Activity 1—Learning About Angling

When one becomes an angler, there are certain things that must be done. Just getting the equipment and heading for the water are not enough. Every angler should make it a point to learn as much as possible. Reading books, magazine articles, and the local newspaper, watching fishing programs on television, and joining an organization devoted to conservation, fishing, or wildlife are excellent methods of learning.

Everyone should read not only modern articles, but also *The Compleat Angler* by Izaak Walton. This book, published in 1653, is a classic on the sport and is interesting reading.

Activity 2—The Financial Impact of Angling

Besides being an enjoyable pastime, sport fishing has a large economic impact. Do you have any idea how much money is involved in fishing in your state?

Write to your State Department of Natural Resources and find out how many fishing licenses are sold each year. Also ask for estimates as to how much money is produced annually by sport anglers. These numbers may make you more aware of the importance of keeping our fishing waters clean and productive.

Activity 3—What is the Ripple Effect

The creation of a new lake or wetland area often provides local flood control and creates habitat for wildlife. However, there can be a sizable economic benefit to a community on a lake. List the *types of businesses* that might profit from the creation of a new fishing area near your town. From this list you will notice that the businesses fall into several categories. Using categories such as food, lodging, gasoline, fishing tackle, groceries, and bait, list as many of the local businesses in your town as you can under each category. How many jobs do they provide? What other businesses benefit from the salaries provided by these jobs? What companies sell goods to the businesses that sell to anglers? This is what is known as the ripple effect. It can have a tremendous effect on the economy of a community.

FISHING SAFELY

Anglers must be prepared to keep safe and comfortable in the outdoors. Fishing isn't a dangerous sport, but it is possible to get caught unexpectedly in bad weather, encounter insects, get a bad case of sunburn, or cut yourself on a fish hook.

Wearing the proper clothing helps to protect you from injury and to keep you warm in cold weather and cool in hot weather. Rainwear can keep you from getting wet and chilled. It is wise to avoid problems by preparing for the unexpected.

SAFETY AROUND WATER

National Safety Council statistics show that drowning is the second leading cause of accidental death (behind auto accidents) for people between the ages of 1 and 44. Most of the 6,000 people who drown

annually were unprepared and never intended to be in the water. Sadly, most drownings occur within a few feet of safety, and most would not occur if personal floatation devices, PFD's, were being worn.

Obviously you will be around water if you are fishing, and accidents can happen. At any moment you can find yourself in the water. A bank can give way, you can slip on a rock, step into a deep hole while wading, or fall out of a boat. Anglers should **learn how to swim and be careful around water at all times**. Even if you know how to swim, the use of the "buddy system" may save your life.

Personal Flotation Devices (PFDs)

Personal flotation devices (PFDs), often called "life vests," are not just for wearing in boats. Anytime you are around deep or fast moving water, **it is**

always best to wear your PFD. U.S. Coast Guard and/or state laws require you to have an approved PFD for each person in a boat. Certain types of boats must also have a cushion or ring that can be thrown to a person in the water.

Types of PFDs. PFDs are rated by type. **Type I PFDs** have the maximum flotation, are designed for rough waters, and will turn an unconscious person's head up and face out of the water to prevent drowning.

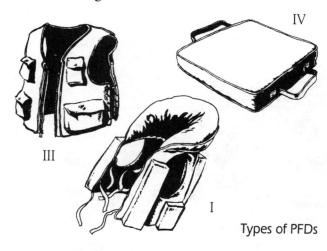

Types of PFDs

Type II PFDs will also turn the wearer to a vertical and slightly backward position to prevent drowning. However, they don't give the long-term protection and flotation that the Type I PFD does.

Type III PFDs are the kind generally sold for recreational use and are favored by anglers. They often have pockets to serve as fishing vests. They will hold the wearer in a face-up position, but will not turn an unconscious person to this position.

Type IV PFDs are designed to be grasped by a person—not worn. These include flotation cushions and rings, which are designed to be thrown to a person who has fallen overboard. All PFD's other than these help to maintain body heat in the water.

Wading. There are several rules you should follow for safe wading:

1. Always wade with another person.
2. Always wear a PFD.
3. Know how deep the water is.
4. Know how strong the current is.
5. Know what the bottom is like.
6. Use a stick or staff and shuffle your feet along the bottom to avoid falling into a hole.

Wading anglers can also wear high-top athletic shoes or wading boots to protect their ankles. Long, lightweight pants can protect from jellyfish and sea nettles in salt water and from snags and rocks in fresh water.

Hip boots or waders keep you dry and protect against the chill of cool water in spring or fall. For cold-weather wading, insulated hip boots or neoprene waders are good.

Reach-Throw-Row-Go. Reach-throw-row-go is a method of rescuing a person who falls overboard or an angler or swimmer in trouble.

The first safety step is to **REACH** out with an oar, tree limb, or other long object if the person is close to you. If you can't reach the angler, then

THROW a life-saving device, such as a flotation cushion or ring. If possible, it should be tied to the end of a line so you can pull the person to you. If a cushion or ring isn't available, anything that floats can be thrown. Ice chests or ski belts can be used in an emergency.

If there's nothing to throw, **ROW** a boat to the person in trouble. There should be someone else in the boat to help pull the victim into the boat. Pulling them in over the stern, or back, of a skiff or johnboat will help avoid upsetting the boat. If the boat has a motor, it must be shut off as you near the person in the water. If the boat is small, have the victim hang onto the side for towing to shore.

Swim out to save the person in trouble *ONLY* as a last resort and *ONLY* if you are an experienced lifeguard or have had life-saving training. **GOing** into the water after the person in trouble is very dangerous. They often panic and injure, or even drown, someone trying to rescue them. **GOing** quickly for help is often the best choice.

Swimming. If you fish, for your own safety, you should know how to swim. During a fishing trip many anglers like to go for a swim for fun or to cool off. Don't swim if there is any doubt about your ability. Never dive into the water of an unknown area and don't swim after a heavy meal. Swimming in cold water can cause hypothermia. Swim only when an experienced swimming partner is with you.

Foul Weather Considerations. Lightning is dangerous. On land, avoid high, isolated structures, such as towers, metal buildings, or single or small groups of trees. Lay down all fishing rods and radios with an antenna, and sit or lie flat. Be especially careful when using graphite fishing rods; they may attract lightning.

SAFETY WITH FISHING EQUIPMENT

Handle your fishing equipment responsibly. Hooks can be particularly dangerous if you do not handle them carefully. Always know where your hook is. Look behind you before you cast to make sure your hook will not be caught on a power line, a tree, or a person.

To avoid hooking yourself, use long-nose pliers to help remove hooks from a fish. If a hook is deep inside the fish, either cut off the line and leave the hook in the fish, or use a hook disgorger. Hooks left in fish will work themselves free or rust out.

When transporting your equipment, remove the hook or lure from your line and store it in your tackle box. If you leave your tackle lying on the ground, others can trip on it and fall, step on a hook, or break your tackle.

FISHING IN WARM WEATHER

Because repeated exposure to too much sun can cause **skin cancer,** your skin must be protected as much as possible. A **sunscreen** lotion should be used to keep the sun's ultraviolet (UV) rays from reaching your skin. One with a Sun Protection Factor (SPF) of 15 on the label gives good protection.

Long pants and long shirt sleeves give you better protection than shorts and short-sleeved shirts. In warm weather, lightweight and light-colored clothing reflects the sun and is cooler. Dark clothing is warmer because it absorbs heat.

Look Before Casting

9

Even in warm weather, it's a good idea to take along a sweater or jacket and rain gear. Even though it may be warm during much of the day, many fishing trips begin early when it's still chilly and end late in the evening when it gets cool.

All anglers should have rainwear. A rain poncho is good, but many anglers prefer a two-piece rain suit with a jacket and pants. Good rainwear is waterproof, not just water-repellent. It should have a full hood to protect your head, a storm flap over the jacket opening, a zipper, snaps or buttons, and elastic around the cuff and ankle openings to keep water out.

Caps and hats are very important, protecting you from glare and against sunburn. Lightweight, light-colored, baseball-style caps are popular among anglers. In tropical areas, such as Florida and the Gulf Coast, some anglers put a cloth on the back of their caps to keep their necks from getting sunburned. Hats also protect your head from hooks on a poor cast.

No one likes to be sunburned, but it happens to most people at some time. Aloe vera and other salves and lotions are the best relief for minor cases of sunburn.

Sunglasses protect your eyes against the sun's glare from the water. Many anglers prefer polarized sunglasses that let them see below the water surface to spot fish and other objects. Some sunglasses have treated lenses to protect eyes from the sun's harmful ultraviolet (UV) light rays.

INSECTS AND INSECT BITES

Insects can be pests. Common ones are mosquitoes, chiggers, ticks, black flies, bees, wasps, and hornets. While you can't avoid insects entirely, there are some things you can do.

1. Try to avoid areas with lots of insects.
2. Don't use cologne, perfume, or other scents that might attract insects.
3. Wear a long-sleeved shirt and long pants.
4. Turn up your shirt collar.
5. Use an insect repellent, but do not get it on your lures or bait since fish can smell it and may not bite.

The best insect repellents include a substance called "DEET." However, because DEET repellents will damage plastic, such as lures and tackle boxes, spread the repellent on by using the back of your hand.

Insect bites and stings can be dangerous. If you have extreme reactions to a sting, carry a special prescription injection kit for such an emergency.

For most people, removing the bee's stinger and applying a pain-killing balm or a paste of baking soda or meat tenderizer will help to relieve the pain and reduce swelling, itching, and inflammation. Always scrape a bee stinger from your skin. Squeezing it and pulling can inject more poison and prolong your discomfort.

FISHING IN COLD WEATHER

If you fish in cold weather, several layers of clothing can keep you warm. Clothing layers trap air between them which provides insulation. If it warms up during the day, you can always take off some of the clothing. In addition to long underwear and warm shirts, jackets and pants, an insulated vest and a rain parka are also good for keeping you warm on cold, windy days. In extremely cold weather, insulated boots and a snowmobile suit are ideal. Warm clothing is especially needed for ice fishing and to avoid hypothermia.

Hypothermia. Hypothermia means your body is losing heat faster than it can produce it. Without treatment, your life is in danger. Exposure to the cold, along with wind, wetness, and exhaustion causes hypothermia. The first symptom is shivering. If not corrected, chilling of the body core causes weakness, hallucinations, uncontrollable limbs, unconsciousness, and finally, death.

Some people think hypothermia only occurs in cold weather, but it can occur in almost any temperature once the body begins to get cold or chilled. Many cases of hypothermia develop in air temperature between 30 and 50 degrees. Cold water takes away body heat 25 times faster than air of the same temperature. Any water colder than 70 degrees can cause hypothermia in an unprotected individual.

H.E.L.P. Position

To protect yourself from hypothermia, stay warm and dry. Remember that wind makes you colder. If you fall into cold water, don't thrash around. Excess movement speeds up heat loss. Instead, bring your knees up toward your chin and bend your legs as though you are sitting. This is called the Heat Escape Lessening Position or **"H.E.L.P."** This helps hold body heat and slows cooling.

To detect hypothermia, watch for these signs:

- Uncontrollable shivering
- Fumbling hands
- Frequent stumbling
- A lurching walk
- Vague slow speech
- Drowsiness or apparent exhaustion

If someone is suffering from hypothermia, immediately call for an ambulance or other medical help. Then, completely remove wet or cold clothing, and replace with warm clothing or place the person in a warm bath, keeping their limbs out of the water. A good substitute is a warm sleeping bag or electric blanket that only covers the head, abdomen, and trunk. Give the victim hot, sweet beverages, but never alcohol. Try to keep the person awake. Don't warm the victim's arms or legs, and don't exercise the victim by walking. This could result in a stroke, a heart attack, even death.

Caps and **hats** are important for preventing loss of body heat from your head-and-neck area. Up to 30 percent of body heat is lost through this area. Headgear used for fishing during the winter should protect most of your head, including your ears. Some good choices are an insulated hat or cap or a wool stocking cap. A scarf can protect your neck.

Fishing is difficult when wearing most gloves. There are gloves, however, that let you tie knots and handle fishing tackle. They include lightweight rubber gloves and "hunter's/angler's gloves," gloves that have a flap so you can expose your fingers. Wool gloves without fingertips are also good.

Ice Fishing. Before fishing on ice, it is a good safety practice to check the thickness of the ice by drilling holes with an ice auger near shore and along your route of travel. Ice has to be at least four inches, and preferably six inches thick, before it is safe for ice fishing. Thinner ice is dangerous because it can break easily.

For ice fishing, use ice creepers or cleated boots to prevent slipping and falling. An ice-fishing sled is good for carrying fishing tackle, thermos bottles, lunch, and a wind shelter or screen.

A snowmobile suit and insulated boots with thick soles are ideal for ice fishing. A warm hat, heavy gloves, and a skier's mask are also needed. Hand warmers are also helpful. A personal flotation device, when worn under clothing, provides extra warmth as well as emergency flotation if you go for an unexpected icy plunge.

BASIC FIRST AID

Removing A Hook From Your Skin. Occasionally an angler will get a fish hook in the skin. Once a fish hook enters the skin beyond its barb, it is difficult to remove. Never remove a hook from around a person's eyes, face, the back of the hands, or any area where ligaments, tendons, or blood vessels are visible. Removing a fish hook is best left to a doctor or a hospital's emergency room.

However, there is a method that can be used to remove a hook if it is not in a vital area. First, cut

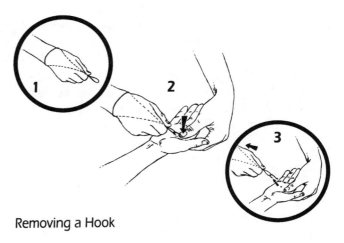

Removing a Hook

the hook away from the rest of the fishing lure. Then, put a loop of heavy twine or fishing line around the bend of the hook. Next, hold down the eye and shank of the hook, pressing it lightly to the skin. Grasp the loop in the line and, with a sharp jerk, pull the hook free.

Any hook wound should be followed by a tetanus shot if the victim has not had one in the past five years.

Cuts and Bleeding. In all cases of serious bleeding where there is a large or deep cut, call a doctor, get the victim to a hospital, or call paramedics at once. Minor cuts can be handled by adhesive bandages and antiseptic. For large or deep cuts, pressing directly on the wound using a clean gauze pad or handkerchief will reduce bleeding. Use the proper procedure taught at Red Cross training courses to ensure that proper amounts of pressure are applied.

CPR. Cardiopulmonary resuscitation, or CPR, is a worthwhile life-saving skill. It is a procedure designed to restore normal breathing to a victim who is not breathing or is having a heart attack. CPR, however, requires special training. CPR training courses are available from the Red Cross.

Other Medical Problems. Snake bites and broken bones are rare but serious emergencies in the outdoors. A person with a broken bone or severe back injury should not be moved until medical help is found. If someone is bitten by a snake, chill the area of the bite with ice. Keep the victim calm and quiet, and immediately take the person to a doctor or hospital.

ACTIVITIES

Activity 1—What Shall I Wear?

Place sheets of different colored construction paper or pieces of clothing in the sun. After five minutes feel each one. Which are the hottest? Coolest? Are the dark colored ones warmer or cooler than the light colored ones? What does this suggest to you about the color of clothing to wear to stay cool while fishing during the summer? What color of clothing would you choose to wear in the winter?

Activity 2—Wet Jeans and Your PFD

Cotton denim, which is the material most jeans are made of, can absorb and hold great amounts of water. The next time you are washing your favorite jeans, stop the washing machine and lift the pants out of the water just enough so that you can feel their weight. How much weight would they add to your body if you were accidently thrown into the water while fishing or boating? Would they make it more difficult to swim? This will illustrate the importance of your PFD.

Activity 3—Watch That Reflection

Place a small mirror in the sun. Angle it toward your arm or hand. Do you feel the intensity of the sun? If the sun is in the right position when you are fishing from a boat, you get reflected sunlight, just like the reflected light from a mirror, which can cause sunburn. You can get sunburned badly in a short time. Always use your sunscreen while fishing.

Activity 4—Saving Your Buddy

Make a list of all the items you could use to rescue a friend while you are fishing, boating, or swimming.

First, list all the items you can think of that you could use to reach out to someone in the water to pull them to shore or to your boat. (These must be things that you would have available during water activities.) Second, list all the floating items which might be available that you could throw to hold a friend up in the water.

CHAPTER 3

SELECTING, MATCHING, AND USING FISHING TACKLE

Fishing tackle can consist of only a handline, hook, bobber, and sinker or can be more complex, like the tackle used for saltwater trolling, or bait or fly casting. Spincast and spinning tackle, while complex in design, is easy to use.

Fishing tackle, with the exception of handlines and cane poles, consists of a reel, rod, line, and terminal tackle. The reel stores enough line, which is your connection to the fish, so fish can "run" after taking the bait or lure. The line must be strong, thin, and have good knot strength. The rod is used to cast the lure or bait to a certain spot and to help the angler fight and land fish.

There are many types of fishing tackle, and each type is designed for a specific purpose. Spincast and spinning tackle is ideal for beginners and for much light-tackle fishing. Other tackle is designed for surf fishing, ocean trolling, fishing for larger species, or fly fishing. You must learn how to select matched tackle for specific fishing conditions.

TACKLE FOR SPECIFIC FISHING CONDITIONS

The first consideration in tackle choice is the species of fish sought. The size, food habits, and depth

13

preferred by the species is critical in choosing tackle. Heavy tackle is recommended for large fish, while light tackle should be used for small fish. Fish that are strong and make long runs must be raised off the bottom with a stout rod and strong line.

Cover and **habitat** are also important considerations in tackle selection. You can use lighter tackle to fish for river smallmouth than fishing for similar size largemouth in brush and log jams. Open-water barracuda can be caught on light tackle while reef-hiding grouper of the same size require heavy tackle.

Food preferences of fish also determine tackle choice. The preference of trout for mayflies, caddis flies, stone flies, and small aquatic insects makes the fly rod ideal for stream fishing. Bottom feeding fish caught by still fishing do not require a rod or reel that will cast well as do fish that strike lures presented by casting. Heavy-action rods are preferred for fish that strike surface lures because the stiff rod allows the angler to work the lure properly.

The kind and type of water also determines tackle selection. Ponds and small streams can be fished with light tackle because they usually contain smaller fish. Offshore saltwater fishing requires the use of large, heavy tackle for the much larger fish.

MATCHED TACKLE

Some anglers say that their fishing tackle must be balanced to work properly. A better way of saying this is to use the word "matched." This is because the word "balanced" doesn't mean how well a rod and reel balances on an angler's finger or in a hand, although that is important for fishing comfort. What it really means is that each element of the entire fishing outfit—rod, reel, line, and lure—is in proper relation to each of the other elements, or matched.

How do you match your tackle? Many anglers choose the rod and reel first and then their lure and line size. It is usually best to work in reverse. The type of fish you seek and the fishing conditions will determine the type and size of the lure or bait. The types and sizes of lures determine what size line should be used. To fish effectively, the line size and lure weight determine the type and size of reel and the necessary rod length and strength. Therefore, using matched tackle means that the rod you use must have an appropriately sized reel, line, and lure. If your tackle is matched, you'll be able to fish more easily, more efficiently, and more effectively.

TYPES OF FISHING TACKLE

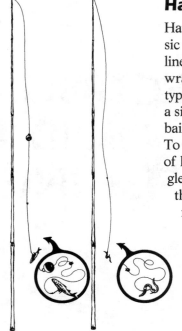

Handlines

Handlines are a very basic way of fishing. A hand line is simply a fishing line wrapped around some type of holder. It may have a sinker and a float with a baited hook on the end. To "cast" a handline, coils of line are held in the anglers hand or placed on the ground and the terminal tackle is tossed out into the water.

Pole and Line

To make a simple fishing outfit, tie one end of a fishing line to the tip of a pole and a hook to the other end of the line. Add a sinker and a bobber and you have a pole and line. The sinker, baited hook, and float are swung out into the water. To make fish landing easy, the line is usually not any longer than the pole. While carrying or storing the pole, the line is wrapped around the pole for security.

Spincasting Tackle

Spincasting tackle is ideal for beginning anglers because it's easy to use and works well. It's the most popular type of fishing equipment in use today.

Reels. A spincasting reel mounts on top of the rod's handle and has a pushbutton to control the line. The fishing line comes through a small hole in the nose cone, a cover on the front of the reel. All spincasting reels store the line on a shallow spool inside the cone. A pickup pin rotates around the front of the spool, picks up the line inside the cone, and coils it on the spool.

Spincasting reels have a drag system that, when set correctly, allows line to be pulled from the reel's spool slowly so the line won't break when a fish is hooked and swims away from you. The drag may be a simple system which is set by a small lever, thumb wheel, or knob on the top or side of the reel, or a

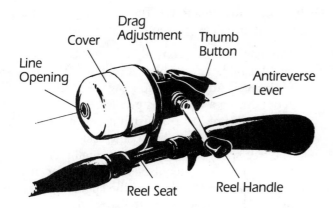

Spincast Reel

star-drag (a star-shaped wheel on the side) that you turn to adjust the drag.

Spincasting reels have an anti-reverse lever which prevents you from turning the handle backward and forces the drag system to slow the line leaving the reel as a fish pulls.

Features of Spincasting Reels. The following are features found on some spincasting reels:

- A ball-bearing drive shaft that is designed to make the reel's performance smoother.
- More than one pickup pin to speed up the retrieval of line.
- An audible alarm or click that sounds when a fish strikes.
- A silent anti-reverse that prevents the handle from turning backward.
- A reversible handle for either right- or left-hand operation.
- A system that "jerks" the fishing line automatically with each turn of the handle to move the lure and entice a fish to strike.

Rods. Spincasting rods have a pistol-type handle, or grip, and line guides on top of the rod. Most rods are 4-1/2 to 6 feet in length and are medium-action for casting 1/4- to 3/4-ounce lures.

Spincasting tackle is best used for smaller fish in fresh water. It's ideal for panfish, small catfish, bass, trout, sauger, and white

Spincast Rod & Reel

bass. Some heavier spincasting tackle, however, is designed for saltwater angling for smaller species of fish.

Spinning Tackle

Spinning tackle can be used for virtually all angling —from fishing for panfish to ocean trolling for big game fish such as marlin and sailfish.

Reels. A spinning reel is often called an "open-face" reel because the spool of fishing line isn't covered. The reel mounts under the rod's handle. These reels range in size from tiny models that weigh only a few ounces to large models designed for saltwater fishing. Some small reels can hold about 165 yards of 4-pound-test line. Large reels can hold 200 yards or more of 20-pound-test line.

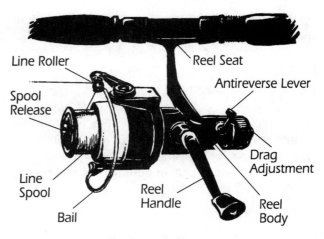

Spinning Reel

Gears turn the wire bail on the front of the reel and cause the spool to move in and out so the line is stored evenly on the spool. The bail usually has a roller on which the line rolls as it is retrieved. This prevents line wear. The bail also flips open for casting and closes automatically when the handle is turned to retrieve the lure.

The spinning reel also has a drag that does the same job as the drag on a spincasting reel, but you adjust it with a knob on either the front or the back of the reel.

Features of Spinning Reels. The following are features found on some spinning reels:

- A ball-bearing line roller to reduce line friction.
- A drive system with one to six ball bearings for smoother performance.

- A reversible handle for either right- or left-hand operation.
- A folding handle to make it easier to store the reel.
- A longer, shallower line spool designed to increase casting distance.
- A trigger mounted over the line spool that lets you pick up the line with your finger and open the bail at the same time for quicker casting.
- A self-centering bail that speeds up casting.

Rods. A spinning rod has a straight handle and large line guides on the bottom of the rod. Most rods range in length from 4 to 6-1/2 feet, but some designed for surf fishing can be 12 feet or longer.

Baitcasting Tackle

Baitcasting tackle is considered more difficult to master than either spincasting or spinning tackle. Baitcasting tackle can be used for all types of fishing.

Reels. Unlike spincast and spinning reels which have line spools that don't turn, casting reels have a revolving spool. A casting reel also has two tension-control systems—one for the spool (cast-control system) and one for the line (the drag system). The spool's cast-control system automatically slows the revolving line spool during a cast.

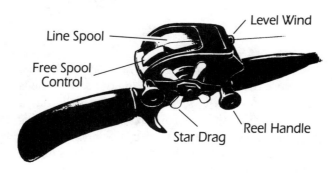

Baitcasting Reel

However, if you fail to slow the spool at the end of a cast by applying pressure with your thumb, line will continue to come off the spool as it revolves. The result is an overrun, or backlash, that will snarl the line on the spool. Improvements in casting reels help prevent line overruns, making modern casting reels easier to use.

Features of Baitcasting Reels. The following are some features found on casting reels:

- The magnetic cast control is controlled with an adjustable knob which is on the left side of the reel. Adjusting it to slow the reel spool during a cast helps prevent line overruns. It must be adjusted according to the weight of lure or bait being cast.
- The free-spool control can be a small push-button or a thumb-controlled bar or lever. It disengages the handle from the spool's gears during the cast, allowing the spool to revolve freely.
- The level-wind is a device that distributes the line evenly on the spool as you retrieve line. The level-wind usually disengages during a cast.
- Many conventional style (revolving spool) boat and trolling reels resemble and work like standard casting reels, but there are some differences. Some have special lever-operated drag systems. They don't have a level-wind or cast controls because they aren't designed for casting.
- Some casting reels have a feature designed for use with a method of fishing called "flipping." This control is usually on top or on the side of the reel. It changes the reel's operation to one in which line can be taken from the spool, and when the control is released, the reel's drag is engaged. Unlike the use of the thumb bar in casting, the free spool does not stay locked in place, but is dependent on constant pressure on the bar.

Rods. A baitcasting rod can have either a pistol-type or a straight handle. Both kinds have a finger, or trigger, grip. As with spincasting tackle, the casting reel mounts on top of the rod. Casting rods have small line guides on top of the rod.

Most casting rods range from 5 to 6-1/2 feet in length, although casting tackle for saltwater and Great Lakes fishing can be 8 feet long or longer. Surf-fishing rods with similar, but larger, casting-style reels may be 12 feet long or longer.

Uses of Baitcasting Tackle. Casting tackle is used for all types of fishing. With ultralight casting tackle, it's possible to cast with lures as light as 1/8 ounce. Heavy tackle can be used for trolling or casting heavy 3-ounce plugs for barracuda, bluefish, musky, and sharks. It can also be used for deep-jigging (fishing vertically with heavy lures) and still-fishing (fishing deep with bait).

Casting tackle is popular for freshwater bass angling, but is also suitable for catfish, carp, salmon, trout, and walleye fishing. Casting tackle also works well for saltwater angling, including surf, pier, and jetty fishing, fishing with bait or lures, vertical fishing over tropical reefs, and some boat trolling.

Casting Baitcasting Tackle. Learning to use casting tackle may take more practice than learning to use spincasting and spinning tackle. Prior to baitcasting you need to adjust the spool tension knob. Tighten it all the way, then hold the rod level and gradually lessen the tension until your plug slowly pulls the line to the ground. This should be done each time you switch to a different weight lure. Follow the steps shown below:

Step 1—Grip the rod by its handle and place your thumb lightly on the line spool. Put the reel in free spool, extend your arm and hold the rod level with the reel handle pointed up. Stand with your body toward the target, but at a slight angle, with your casting arm closest to the target. **Step 2**—Swiftly and smoothly, using just one motion, bend your casting arm at the elbow and raise your casting arm until your casting hand is almost at eye level. **Step 3**—When the rod is almost vertical, it will be bent by the weight of the plug. As the rod bends, move your forearm forward with a slight wrist movement. **Step 4**—When the rod reaches a one o'clock position, lift your thumb slightly off the line, but keep light contact with it. As the plug nears the target, gently brake the unwinding spool with your thumb. Follow through by lowering the rod to follow the flight of the lure. Using your thumb, brake the spool to a complete stop the instant the lure reaches its destination. **Step 5**—Switch the rod to your other hand, gripping the rod in front of the reel. Turn the reel handle with your opposite hand to retrieve the lure. If the lure landed close in front of you, your thumb released the line too late. If the plug went more or less straight up, you released your thumb too soon.

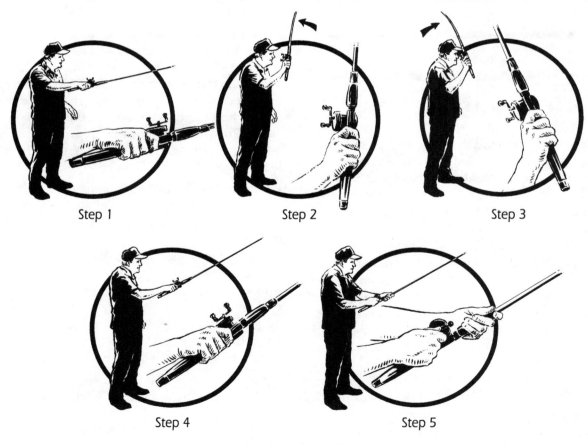

Step 1

Step 2

Step 3

Step 4

Step 5

Casting Baitcasting Tackle

Flyfishing Tackle

Flyfishing tackle is different from all other types. In flyfishing, the line is most important because the line is cast—not the lure or fly. With other fishing tackle the bait or lure is cast and its weight pulls the line from the reel.

In flycasting, the angler casts long loops of line forward and backward in the air until the fly reaches the target during a forward cast.

Fly Lines. Fly lines vary in construction or shape. Because they are made with a plastic coating over a braided core, they can be adjusted to different shapes, or tapers.

A fly line that has the same thickness from one end to the other is called a **level line**. This is the lowest-cost line and is suitable for beginners and simple fishing. A **double-taper** line has a long, level center section, which tapers down to a thin section at each end. A **weight-forward line** is the most popular line because it makes long casts easier than level and double-taper lines.

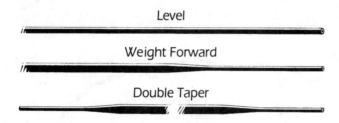

Level

Weight Forward

Double Taper

Fly Line Tapers

For more experienced flyfishing anglers, there are special lines. One is called the **shooting head** for anglers who need to cast longer distances. It is usually about 30 feet long and similar to the weight-forward taper. But instead of the thicker tapered section of a standard line, the shooting head is attached to a "shooting line," which is really a level, fine-diameter fly line or nylon line. In addition, there are lines designed for fishing various species of fish, including bass, steelhead, bonefish, and tarpon.

Fly lines also vary in their ability to **float** or **sink**. Most are designed to float because most flyfishing is done close to the water's surface. Some lines have neutral buoyancy (they suspend just under the surface) while others sink at different speeds. Another kind of fly line sinks at the end while the rest floats.

Matching Fly Tackle. Like other fishing tackle, fly fishing tackle must be matched to work well. A certain weight fly line should be used with a rod and reel made for that weight line. The American Sportfishing Association (ASA) has developed a standard system that is used by line makers.

Fly line weights range from 1 through 15 with 4–5 weight commonly used for trout and panfish and 7–8 weight for bass, larger trout, and small salmon. Because it's the line that casts the fly, the key to line-weight selection is the size, weight, and wind resistance of the fly you plan to use.

Fly line packages are labeled with some of the following codes:

L (level), **DT** (double taper), **WF** (weight forward),
ST (shooting taper), **F** (floating), **S** (sinking),
F/S (floating/sinking), and a number 3 through 12 (weight of the line).

For example, a line labeled "**WF7F**" means it is weight-forward, 7-weight, floating line.

Most fly lines are about 80 feet long—long enough for most fishing. However, many anglers add a backing line behind the fly line as insurance against long-running fish.

Fly Fishing Leaders. Because thick fly line cannot be tied to the tiny eye of a hook or a fly and because it might spook a fish, a long, thin nylon leader is tied to the front end of the fly line. Most leaders are also tapered just like fly lines. The leader tapers from a heavy end, often about 30-pound-test, to a "tippet" of 1- to 10-pound test, depending on the fly and type of fishing. Leaders range from 7-1/2 to 12 feet in length for most fishing.

Fly Rods. The fly rod has a straight handle. The fly reel is mounted under the handle at the very end of the rod. The rod is held so that the guides are under the rod.

Because the line is cast, the best action is one that is often called "parabolic," that is, bending smoothly from the tip to close to the grip. Fly rods vary in strength or power (corresponding to the weight of the fly line) and also length. Most rods range in length from 7 to 10 feet. Because of their length, most are two-piece.

Fly Fishing Reels. During a cast, the fly reel isn't used. When a fish is hooked, some anglers use the reel's drag to fight a fish, while others prefer to retrieve the line—and fish—by hand.

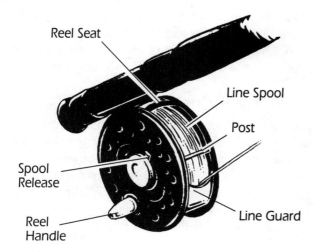

Reel Seat

Line Spool

Post

Spool
Release

Line Guard

Reel
Handle

Fly Casting Reel

Types Of Fly Reels. There are three basic types of fly reels. The **single-action** reel is little more than a spool in a frame. It's called "single action" because one turn of the handle causes the spool to make one turn.

The **multiplying-action** reel has gears where one turn of the handle causes several turns of the spool.

The **automatic** reel has springs and gears along with a trigger that causes the reel to retrieve line automatically when the trigger is pulled.

Fly reels come in different sizes to hold different size lines. Some large models are designed for big-game fishing and large fish and have special drag systems.

Casting Fly Fishing Tackle. Flycasting doesn't involve the reel—only the rod and line. To practice, tie on a piece of yarn instead of a hook. To begin, hold the handle in front of the reel with the reel below the rod. Align the thumb of your casting hand with the rod and place it as nearly on top of the handle as your can. Bend your wrist forward until the rod becomes a parallel extension of your forearm. The perfect casting stroke takes place between the 1 o'clock position in front of you and the 11 o'clock position, slightly behind your head. Since this area of movement is relatively slight, there is a tendency to let the wrist do all the work, often resulting in an exaggerated,

crooked arc. The entire hand must travel in a nearly straight line with a slight upward lift through the back cast and a slight overhead movement on the forward cast. For a basic cast, follow the steps shown below:

Step 1—With the rod at a 2 o'clock position, pull about 20 feet of line off the reel through the rod, onto the ground. Then pull off another 15–20 feet of slack line between the first guide (the stripper guide) and the reel. Coil this line in your free hand. **Step 2**—With a smooth, even liftoff, begin your back cast. Don't jerk. A slow-starting, rapidly-accelerating movement will pick up the line smoothly. **Step 3**—As the rod passes the 1 o'clock point, speed up the backward motions and flip the line up and back, stopping the rod abruptly at 11 o'clock. Open your wrist enough to allow the rod to drift back with the weight of the line. Overcome the feeling that the line will fall unless you start the forward

Casting Fly Fishing Tackle

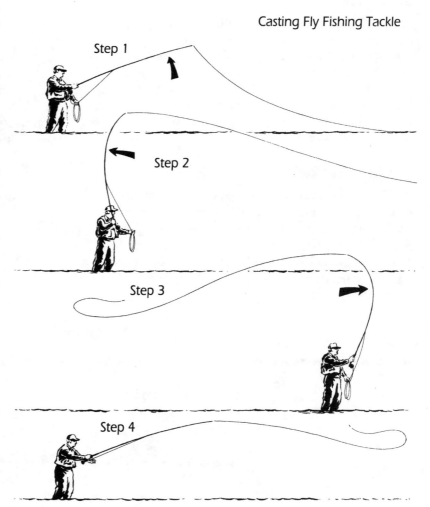

Step 1

Step 2

Step 3

Step 4

cast instantly. Take a pause, and even turn your head to watch as the line loops and rolls out behind you. As the back cast rolls out to its end, begin the forward cast. Stop the rod at 1 o'clock and then let your hand and rod follow through with the casting stroke. **Step 4**—As you follow through and the weight of the cast line begins to pull, let the slack line from your hand be pulled through the line guides to extend your cast.

As you practice, you'll learn that your line hand plays an important role. It is part of the line retrieval system; it helps keep tension on the line when a fish strikes; and it holds the slack line as you attempt longer casts.

The line hand is also used during the "false cast." This is an incomplete cast repeated a number of times to increase the amount of line that is finally cast.

Surf Tackle

Surf tackle is heavy. Long, stiff rods, ranging in length from 9 to 14 feet, allow the angler to make long casts with heavy lures. The long rods also hold the line up above the breakers, which would otherwise catch the line and drag the bait. Surf tackle can be either spinning or revolving spool style, although most anglers fish the easier-to-use spinning style.

Trolling Tackle

Trolling tackle is also heavy tackle, either spinning or casting, in which 6-1/2 to 8-foot rods are used with large reels that have great line capacity. Trolling tackle is used to trail a lure or bait behind the boat. Usually the rods are held in rod holders and have long handles. Line test is usually heavy.

In salt water, many anglers use lines that correspond to tournament and record "line classes" from 8- to 130-pound line. The rods are relatively short to allow for leverage in fighting hooked fish.

Saltwater Tackle

Saltwater tackle must be made of noncorrosive material because saltwater will corrode any aluminum, steel or iron parts. The metal parts of saltwater tackle usually are made of stainless steel or nickel chrome. Saltwater tackle ranges from the ultralight equipment used in inshore fishing to the extremely large and heavy tackle for deep sea fishing.

Ice Fishing

Ice fishing is a very specialized sport. One- to three-foot rods are most often used. Simple reels are used to hold the line. Ice fishing can also be done with tip-ups. Tip-ups fit over a hole in the ice. When a fish hits, it releases a lever. This causes a flag to tip up, alerting the angler.

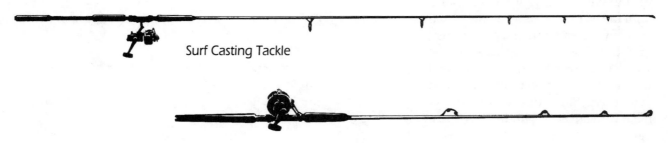

Saltwater Tackle

Surf Casting Tackle

Heavy Trolling Tackle

TACKLE MAINTENANCE

If you take good care of your fishing tackle, it will last a long time. Fishing tackle should be used only for activities for which it is designed and, when not in use, should be properly stored.

Rods

Fishing rods are designed for casting, trolling and fighting fish, not for retrieving snagged lures or use as a boat pole. When rods are not being used, placing them in a rod rack, either in a boat or at home, will help keep them from being damaged. Both rods and reels should be washed with fresh water after fishing, especially if you have been fishing in salt water.

Reels

A reel's drag should be set prior to fishing, and then loosened when you are finished, to preserve the soft drag washers. Reels need to be oiled and greased periodically following the manufacturer's instructions. Once each year, a reel should be taken to a reel service center for cleaning, or if you can do the job, dismantled for cleaning at home.

Lures

Lures should be kept in tackle boxes, but placing too many lures in a compartment can cause hooks to scratch the finish of other lures. Soft-plastic lures, such as worms and grubs or lures with plastic or rubber skirts, should be kept separate from metal or hard-plastic lures. Different types of plastics can react and harm the lures. Soft lures should also be separated by color or they may discolor each other.

Tackle boxes should be stored open until wet fishing tackle is dry. An electric hair dryer can be used to speed up the drying process.

Other Tackle

Other tackle also requires care. Nets should be checked for holes. Rubber fishing gear such as boots, hipboots, or waders should be hung or folded in a bag and stored in a cool, dark place. Tackle boxes need to be emptied and periodically cleaned.

Giving attention to the care and maintenance of fishing tackle will help to insure that it works so you don't lose the big one! In addition, it will save you money.

ACTIVITIES

Activity 1—Becoming Familiar With Different Types of Tackle

Examine the four major types of fishing tackle at your fishing tackle store. Examine spincasting and spinning tackle. Notice how a spincast reel sits on top of the rod and the rod has its line guides on top of the rod, whereas the spinning outfit has the reel and the guides on the bottom. Examine tackle from several different companies, noting likenesses and differences.

Now look at bait casting tackle. Notice the revolving spool and the level wind. Find the "star" drag and the free-spool control.

See how a flycasting reel is at the extreme end of the rod and how you cast with your hand above the reel. Also notice the length of the rod in comparison to the other rods you have examined.

A sales clerk will be glad to speak with you concerning the use of each type of equipment. Talk with the clerk about matched tackle. After this discussion you will be able to determine which type of equipment you are most comfortable with for the type of fishing you plan to do.

Activity 2—Practice Casting

Place a piece of cardboard in your yard, driveway, or other safe place. Take your fishing outfit with a practice plug without hooks. Stand about 25 feet away and practice casting by aiming at the cardboard target. Practice until you can hit the target regularly. To make a game of this, count three points for each cast that hits the target and one point for each cast that hits the ground and bounces onto the target. How many casts did you have to make to score 25 points? 50 points? 100 points?

TERMINAL TACKLE, LINE, BAITS, LURES, AND ACCESSORIES

TERMINAL TACKLE

Fish Hooks

Fish hooks come in a large variety of sizes and styles. Hooks are made with single, double, or treble (three) points. Each style has a special name and its own shape, shank thickness, shank length, and point style.

Hook sizes range from size 22 (very small and used for tying flies) through size 1 in even sizes (22, 20, 18, 16, 14, 12, 10, 8, 6, 4, 2, and 1), and in

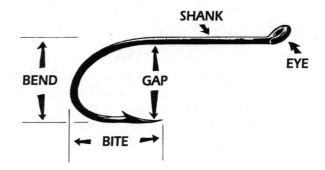

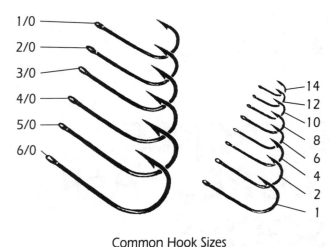

Common Hook Sizes

larger sizes, from 1/0 (smallest of the /0 sizes) through size 16/0 in both odd and even sizes.

Hooks vary in other features, too. Their **points** can be straight or curved and barbed or without barbs. Certain waters require barbless hooks. Hook **bends** vary from a half-round shaft (perfect bend) to a variety of bends for special-purpose fishing.

| Pike | Bent Down | Beak Point | Cam-Action |

Specialty Hooks

Some have hooks twisted sideways so that the point is not in line with the shank. Hook **eyes** can be round, tapered, or in some other shape.

Some hooks have bait-holding devices. The most common bait-holder is a series of slices on the hook shank, while some treble hooks have springs around the shank to hold prepared baits.

Hooks come in a variety of finishes, including bronze, gold, nickel, cadmium, silver, and black. Some saltwater hooks are made of stainless steel to prevent them from rusting. Hooks often need to be sharpened before use and resharpened while using.

FISHING LINE

The most widely used fishing line is made of nylon, called monofilament. It is ideal for most casting, trolling, still fishing, drifting, or other fishing that uses spincasting, spinning, casting, trolling, and surf tackle.

Braided dacron line is often used for trolling for big game fish or when little line stretch is desired. In addition, wire or lead core line is also used for deep trolling because its weight can get a lure deeper.

Lines come in many colors. Most nylon lines are designed so fish won't see them in the water. Anglers still argue about which is the best color or shade to use.

Fishing line comes in a variety of sizes, or strengths, called **pound-test**. All lines—nylon, Dacron, and wire —come in strengths that vary from one- to 200-pound test. The most popular nylon lines range from six- to 20-pound test.

Fishing Knots. Knots are the weakest link in a fishing line so you want to tie the strongest knots possible. To tie a knot properly:

- Keep twists and spirals uniform.
- Snug knots slowly and tightly, using steady even pressure.
- Wet the knot to help draw it up smoothly; this reduces friction, which weakens the line.
- Trim the tag end of the line carefully, leaving at least 1/8 inch from the knot.

The **Improved Clinch Knot** is a popular knot for nylon line up to 20-pound test. It's used to connect line to terminal tackle.

The **Palomar Knot** is easier to tie than the Improved Clinch Knot except when using large lures. It, too, is used for connecting line to terminal tackle.

The **Loop Knot** is used for minnow type baits and diving lures. The loop attached to the lure allows the lure to move more freely.

The **Blood Knot** can be used for connecting monofilament line to leaders.

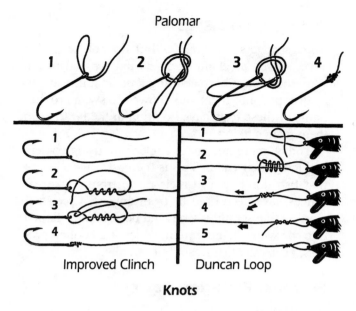

Palomar

1   2   3   4

1   2   3   4   1   2   3   4   5

Improved Clinch   Duncan Loop

Knots

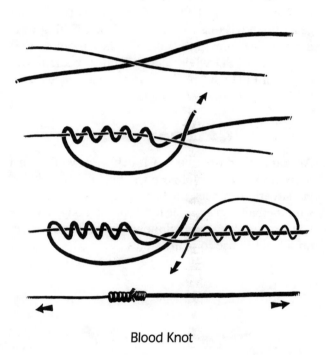

Blood Knot

There are many other fishing knots that anglers find useful. These are illustrated in booklets prepared by major manufacturers of fishing line. To find one of these booklets, check your local tackle dealer or visit the exhibit booths of line manufacturers at fish, sport, and outdoor shows.

SINKERS AND FLOATS

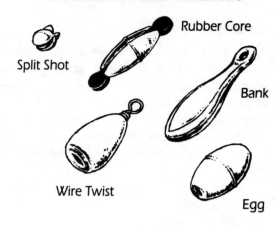

Split Shot   Rubber Core

Bank

Wire Twist

Egg

Sinkers

A sinker is a weight designed to keep a bait down in the water. Like hooks, sinkers come in a variety of weights, sizes, shapes, and styles. Some sinkers, such as the pyramid and bank styles, are used to hold baited hooks on the bottom. Sinkers such as wire twists, split-shot, pinch-on, and rubber-core sinkers fasten to fishing line.

Bobbers

Surface floats, or bobbers, are designed to keep a baited hook at the depth you want to fish. They also help you know when you have a strike. Use a bobber that's just large enough to keep your bait and sinker from pulling it under the water. Pencil-style bobbers are more sensitive than round ones. Because of this, it is easier to tell if a fish is biting, but round bobbers are easier to cast. Slip bobbers, which are available in both round and

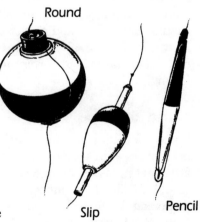

Round

Slip   Pencil

pencil styles, are easy to cast because very little line is below the bobber during the cast. Bobbers can be easily adjusted to allow you to fish different depths. This is important when fish are suspended at a particular depth between the surface and the bottom. Crappie, a species favored by many anglers, often suspend.

ACCESSORIES

Tackle Boxes

Fishing hooks, lures, and other equipment should be organized so you can find an item easily. Some boxes are ideal for small lures, some for large lures, and others for certain types of lures such as spinnerbaits, jigs and pork rind, or plugs. Many plastic baits such as worms can erode plastic tackle boxes. The one you purchase should be resistant to this deterioration.

There are also "soft" tackle boxes which are made of some durable material like nylon and contain pockets for storing lures.

Landing Nets and Gaffs

Landing nets and gaffs make landing fish easier. The disadvantage of using gaffs is that they injure fish so they can't be returned to the water. Gaffs are more commonly used in saltwater fishing. You should select your landing net for the kind of fishing you plan to do. A "soft" net that will not injure a fish's slime layer is important for catch-and-release fishing.

Hand Tools

Some hand tools are necessities for fishing. Long-nose pliers with wire cutters and a hook disgorger are often necessary. Fingernail clippers are needed to cut fishing line rather than using your teeth. A pocket knife is needed to cut both line and bait. Small screwdrivers, reel oil, and a reel tool are necessary for adjusting a reel. Biodegradable soap is needed to wash outboard motor oil, gas, or fish or bait slime from your hands. A hand towel is mandatory.

Anglers who keep their fish also need fish-cleaning tools such as a fillet knife, a fish scale, a skinning board, and skinning pliers.

Stringers and Bags

Rope stringers are popular but do not keep fish alive as well as chain or safety-pin type stringers. Wire mesh bags have a spring-type lid and fish can be dropped into them and allowed to swim around. Some of these bags have flotation in the lid to keep them from sinking.

Today, more and more anglers are using coolers and icing their catch. This is the best way to insure that fish don't spoil. Creels made from wicker or canvas have been used by trout anglers. Creels are worn with a shoulder strap and occasionally dipped into the water. Evaporation, which is a cooling process, keeps the fish fresh, but not alive.

Personal Flotation Device

A personal flotation device (PFD), also known as a life jacket, should be part of your essential fishing gear. It's advisable to wear one when fishing near deep or fast moving water. The law requires that you have a PFD when fishing from a boat. If you choose a PFD with pockets, you can also use it as a fishing vest to hold your tackle.

NATURAL BAITS

As you learn more about fish behavior, you'll learn more about how to choose the best bait for different situations. Check the fishing regulations to make sure the bait you select is legal for the body of water you are fishing. Live minnows and other live fish are illegal to use in many states.

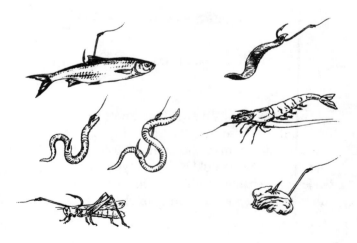

Good saltwater baits include sea worms, eels, crabs, shrimp, strips of squid and cut up pieces of fish. Some of the best baits for freshwater fishing include worms, leeches, minnows, crayfish, crickets and grasshoppers. Other freshwater natural baits include frogs, fish eggs, and cut up parts of fish.

Besides natural baits there are many prepared baits such as doughballs and stinkbait for carp and cat-fish. Unused live bait should never be dumped into the water. It may not be native to the lake or stream, and if introduced, could cause many problems.

Natural Baits

BAIT	SPECIES	HOW TO HOOK	COMMENTS
Worms	Excellent for most fresh and saltwater fish	Insert hook through the side of small worms at several places; for bait-stealing fish, thread the worm on the hook	Worms range in size from small manure worms to large nightcrawlers; keep cool and moist
Minnows	Excellent for most fresh and saltwater fish	Hook through both lips; through the back at the dorsal fin; or by running the line through the body and inserting hook in the tail	Includes chubs, daces, shiners; can be obtained at bait shops; keep cool in fresh water
Insects	Especially good for panfish	Land insects can be hooked once through the body or tied to the hook with fine copper wire	Land insects are: crickets, grasshoppers, and grubs, gall worms and caterpillars. Water insects include hellgrammites, caddis flies and mayflies
Bait Leeches	Excellent bait for many fish, including walleye	Hook through sucker in the tail	
Sea Worms (Blood Worms)	Excellent for almost all inshore saltwater fish	Can be used whole or in pieces on a hook	Because they can bite, care is needed in handling them
Clams, Mussels, & Scallops	Good for perch, drum, sea trout and rockfish	Thread on hook	Must be removed from their shells; small cut-up pieces of clam are used on smaller hooks
Whelks and Conchs	Good for bonefish, snapper, and grouper	Thread on a hook	Used in southern areas for tropical fish

PREPARED BAITS

For bottom-feeding fish like carp and catfish, bread, small pieces of cheese, and canned corn are good. You can also buy commercially made baits. Many anglers, however, like to make their own bait for these fish. Here are two recipes to make bait to catch bottom feeding fish:

CARP DOUGHBALLS

1. Mix 1 cup of flour, 1 cup of yellow cornmeal, and 1 teaspoon of sugar in a bowl.
2. Take a 1-quart container of water and pour just enough of it into the mixture to make a heavy dough.
3. Roll the dough into balls about 1/2-inch to 1-inch in diameter.
4. Mix the rest of the water with 1 cup of molasses and pour it into a pan.
5. Put the pan on the stove and bring the molasses and water to a boil.
6. When the mixture is boiling, drop in several doughballs, but don't overcrowd them. Cook them or 2 to 3 minutes.
7. Cook the rest of the doughballs, a few at a time, in the same way.

You can store the cooked doughballs in the leftover water and molasses.

When using doughballs or stinkbait, use small treble hooks. A treble hook has three points. Some have a spring wrapped around the shank to help hold the bait.

Many manufacturers make "stinkbaits." Homemade stinkbait can be made using the following recipe.

CATFISH STINKBAIT

1. Fill a jar with pieces of a forage fish such as shad.
2. Cover the jar with the lid, but leave the lid loose so gases will escape.
3. Put the jar in direct sunlight for a day or two.

When you open the jar, you'll know your catfish "stinkbait" is ready to use.

ARTIFICIAL LURES

Fishing lure companies make lures in many sizes, styles, colors, and patterns. The instructions that come with a lure can help you learn how to use it most effectively.

Jigs

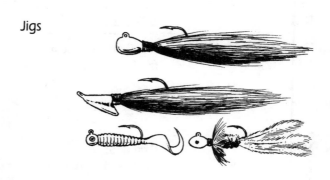

Spoons

Plugs

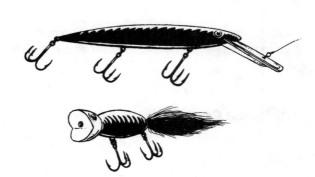

Artificial Lures

LURE TYPE	SPECIES	DESCRIPTION	COMMENTS
Jigs	Attractive to nearly all fish in both fresh and saltwater	Have a heavy head with the hook molded into the head; most are dressed with animal hair, soft plastic bodies, feathers, rubber or other material	A minnow or pork rind is often used with a jig
Spoons	Designed to look like a swimming baitfish and can be used for both fresh and saltwater fishing	Many different weights, sizes, shapes and colors	Can be trolled, jigged, and cast; great variation in size. Jigging spoons are usually slimmer than casting or trolling spoons; jigging spoons are designed to be fished near the bottom
Plugs	Used for nearly all species of fish	Body is usually made of wood or hard plastic; many have a special plate or cupped face for surface use; others have a "lip" that makes them dive to different depths	Can be cast or trolled. Range in size from small 1/8-ounce to large salt water and musky models 12-inches long; available in many colors for different types of fishing
Spinners	Attractive to many species of fish	Have one or more blades that spin around a straight wire shaft	Many are "dressed" with animal hair, feathers, colored beads, or other materials; variety of sizes and weights
Spinnerbaits	Attractive to many fish species	A lure with one or more blades that spin around a "safety-pin" type shaft; the hook is molded into the head	Some have skirts made from animal hair, rubber, vinyl, or other materials; variety of sizes, colors, blades, and finishes; single and double-blade models are common

Spinners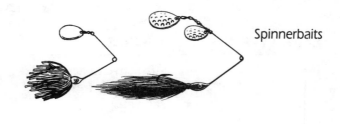

Spinnerbaits

Other Lures

Other lures used in fishing include buzzbaits that are designed to create noise on the surface; soft-plastic lures such as worms, minnows, and grubs; and poppers and flies for flyfishing. In addition, there are lures that are difficult to categorize because they combine elements of several lure types (for example, a jig with a spinner, or a spoon, spinner, or propeller blade with a floating plug body). Live bait can be added to some lures to make them more attractive to the fish.

Plastic Baits

Poppers and Flies

As you understand more about the environment fish live in and how they behave, you will learn which bait or lure is best for specific fish during different seasons of the year.

ACTIVITIES

Activity 1—Building A Worm Motel

Earthworms are one of the most common and effective baits used. They can be raised quite easily.

Build a rectangular form of 2" x 10" treated lumber 30 inches by 60 inches and 20 inches high. Fill it with good dirt mixed with peat moss.

Collect or buy several dozen night crawlers and put them into the bin. Sprinkle with water to keep the top 12–15 inches of soil damp, and cover with cardboard placed directly on the soil.

Feed by spreading alfalfa pellets on the soil and covering again with the cardboard. Keep the soil moist so that the worms won't go deep, and replace the cardboard as it decomposes and is used by the worms. Within a few weeks, you will find you have a constant and easily obtained bait source. You might even find a bait store that will take some of the excess off your hands.

Activity 2—Friction and Tying Strong Knots

You may have read that monofilament line can be weakened by heat generated from friction. Tying knots while your line is dry creates friction which weakens your line. Here is a good demonstration to show that.

Tie a piece of monofilament line to a table leg or another stationary object. Pull the line taut and grab it between your thumb and forefinger. Run your dry fingers up and down the line several times while squeezing. Now untie the line and pull on it, trying to break it. Notice how easily it breaks. Take another piece of the same line, and wetting your fingers, follow the same procedure. Try to break this line. It is more difficult.

Now you know why you should wet the line when you pull knots up tight.

Activity 3—Knot Tying

Find a piece of heavy twine or thin clothesline rope and a bolt with a big eye to represent the hole in a hook. Practice tying the knots mentioned in this chapter until you can tie these knots without looking at the directions. Practice with monofilament line after you have learned how to tie these knots with the rope.

Activity 4—Know How Your Lures Work

Successful fishing requires the proper presentation of lures. One way to be more successful is to know just what each lure does under varying methods of presentation and retrieval. To better know your lures, watch how they react in the water.

Using a swimming pool, bath tub, or any clear body of water, retrieve lures at varying speeds. Take note of their action at each speed. A little time spent here will benefit you later in waters where you can't see the lures.

CHAPTER 5

LOCATING FISH

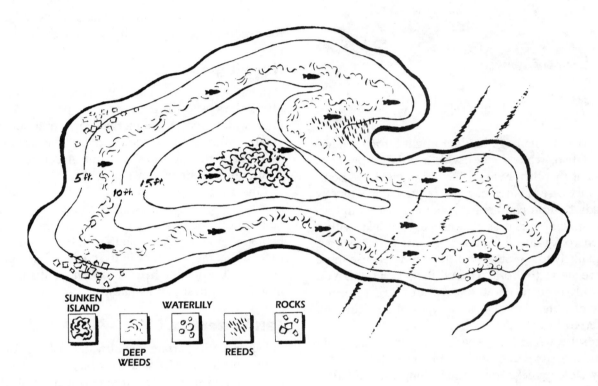

SUNKEN ISLAND

DEEP WEEDS

WATERLILY

REEDS

ROCKS

Fish tend to concentrate in certain areas, depending on the species and the environment in which they live. Where fish can be found depends on the season, available food supplies, the water's oxygen content, water temperature, light levels, the type of bottom, and schooling tendencies of different species. You'll learn about these elements later in the manual.

To locate a species of fish, it's important to learn its special needs and preferences. Your chance of locating and catching a certain species is directly proportional to what you know about that species. For example, salmon and trout require water with higher oxygen and lower temperature levels than bass. They also prefer a different habitat and relate to the bottom and other structures near food and migration paths.

READING THE WATER

Your fishing success will be increased if you learn to determine what is under the water's surface. Anglers often call this "reading the water." It simply means using knowledge and experience to determine what is under the water and what species of fish may be located there.

Structure

Structure is nothing more than something unusual on the bottom or in the water around which fish will tend to gather. If the structure is unusually large, isolated, or different in some way, it will attract more fish than a structure that is more common. For example, in a bay with dozens of stumps, there

33

are likely to be largemouth bass present, but they will be widely spread out among the stumps. However, in a bay with only a small group of stumps, the bass would likely be bunched near the stumps.

Fish Near Structure

In rivers, one large boulder might attract a number of fish, while a pool with a number of rocks could attract fish, but not like the single, large boulder. Likewise, an area of rocks or gravel on a mostly muddy bottom can create structure that would attract smallmouth bass or walleye. In a lake with a mixed rocky and mud bottom, carp or catfish are more likely to be found over the mud because these fish relate to the forage found in soil or sand. You not only need to know the types of structure in a body of water, but also what types of structure are preferred by specific species.

In saltwater fishing, examples of structure could include oyster bars, shoals, pilings, docks, piers, buoys, old wrecks, and other things. Ocean fish, like dolphin, are attracted to floating material, so anglers often troll past any flotsam they spot.

Still Waters

Still waters are the most difficult waters to "read," or interpret, because the calm surface offers no clues as to the water's depth or what features may be present on the bottom.

Often, the best way to read a pond, lake, or reservoir is to look closely at the surrounding land. Except for manmade changes, the type of bottom (soil, rock, and other material) is likely to be the same as found on shore in the same area. The presence of water plants such as lily pads or cattails indicates shallow areas. In manmade ponds and lakes, the deepest areas are usually near the dam.

Running Waters

Waters with a current are easier to read. Current offers clues as to the depth and the presence of any underwater objects. Submerged rocks and boulders create swirls on the water's surface. The size of the swirls is relative to the size of the structure and its depth under water.

Objects in the water—rocks, stumps, pilings, docks, piers, buoys, and other things—are important to note because they have a "cushion" of water behind them that allow fish to rest, but still be close to food that may move by in the current. Such places are ideal locations to fish for catfish, panfish, smallmouth bass, trout, and walleye.

Salt Water

Structure is important in saltwater fishing for the same reasons. Species such as cobia, perch, sea bass, sea trout and striped bass frequent such areas. Both inshore currents and bay and estuary tidal flows cause strong currents similar to those in rivers. These tidal currents reverse themselves each day as water levels rise or fall. When the water moves toward shore, it is called the **flood current**. When it flows seaward, it is called the **ebb current**.

The best places to fish are often around obstructions or currents on the down-current side where fish can lie in protected water, yet easily reach food that moves by. The down-current side of any obstruction reverses each time the tide changes. Many anglers feel that incoming tides are better fishing as well as safer.

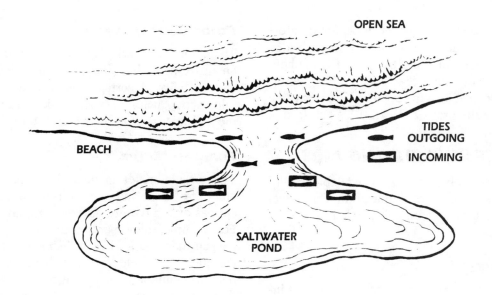

OPEN SEA

BEACH

TIDES
OUTGOING
INCOMING

SALTWATER
POND

LOCATING A FISHING SPOT

There are a number of ways to mark a good fishing spot so that you can return to it later. The simplest way to mark a spot is to take visual sightings of two landmarks in separate locations on shore. For best results, the landmarks should be as close to right angles as possible. For example, two tall pine trees on shore in line with the spot and two telephone poles at a right angle in line with the same spot will provide an accurate sighting. Then, it is possible to follow one line of landmarks—the pine trees, for instance—until the line made by the second landmarks—the telephone poles—is intersected.

Cross-Triangulation

To find a spot at a certain depth, depth soundings can be taken with a measured, weighted line if you don't have an electronic depthfinder.

Maps and Charts

Maps are drawings of a land area that often include rivers, ponds, and lakes. Some of the most useful maps show the area of a manmade body of water before it was formed. Thus, they show the contours of the bottom (roads, creeks, building foundations, and railroad beds). However, some map makers do include bottom depths, type of structure, fishing spots, and manmade objects that attract fish.

Charts, meanwhile, show a water area and some of the surrounding land. Charts are usually made of larger bodies of water. They are available for all of the coastal areas and the Great Lakes. Charts show bottom depth, structure, reefs, courses (compass readings from ports to fishing spots), channels, and piers.

To use a map or chart, an angler must orient the map properly by using a compass to line up magnetic north, as shown on the compass, with north as shown on the map or chart. By doing this, the direction to fishing areas can be determined from the dock, and this course can be followed with the compass.

When using a map or chart, look for features favored by the species for which you plan to fish. For example, if you're after largemouth bass, look for shallow areas, stump fields, standing timber, weedy shoreline areas, breaklines (a sharp drop-off in depth), creek beds, and similar areas. For walleye, locate deep rocky areas, often near running water, such as the mouth of a creek.

For coastal saltwater species, look for comfort zones where fish can hide, such as pilings, bridge abutments, docks, shoals, bars, buoys, reefs, or fathom lines for free-swimming ocean species. For migrating fish like bluefish, fish the open water areas while trying to locate the prey on which these fish feed.

ELECTRONIC FISHING AIDS

A number of electronic devices are available to help anglers find fish. Some are simple and inexpensive; others are expensive and are only needed for fishing from large boats.

Depthfinders

The depthfinder, or sonar, is an instrument that indicates the bottom's depth.

One kind of depthfinder is called a "flasher" because it has a small light that rotates rapidly around a dial and flashes to indicate the depth and if fish are present. With experience, an angler can also determine the type of bottom and the presence of brush or other cover on the bottom.

The chart, or graph recorder, is another kind of depthfinder. It shows the depth while drawing a picture of everything on the bottom and any fish between the surface and the bottom.

LCD Unit

Newer depthfinders work much like the chart recorder, but show the information on a liquid-crystal-display (LCD) screen instead of paper. Most show the information in tiny black blocks, called "pixels," which stands for "picture elements." More expensive models use color.

There are also video depthfinders that show their information in one or several colors.

Color (Light) Meter

The color meter, which is actually a light meter, is an instrument that measures the amount of light and visibility of certain colors in the water. This information helps an angler select a lure with the most visible color in the water at different depths.

Oxygen Meter

The oxygen meter is helpful in determining the amount of dissolved oxygen in the water. Different species of fish require different amounts of oxygen. For example, salmon and trout need higher levels of oxygen than species like catfish and carp. The oxygen meter can help you find these levels and also help you eliminate areas in a body of water where there may not be enough oxygen for fish.

pH Meter

The pH meter measures, on a scale that runs from 0 to 14, the alkalinity or acidity in water. It helps an angler determine if the water has a pH reading that is suited for fish. The best fishing for many game fish is usually found close to the middle of the scale, or 7.0 pH. Water that is too acidic (less than 7.0 pH) or too alkaline (more than 7.0 pH) may not attract fish, though many species can tolerate pH levels between 4.0–9.0.

Temperature Meter

A temperature meter measures water temperature and they are often built into boats. Some meters have a sensor on the end of a wire so an angler can record water temperature at various depths.

The reason for measuring water temperature is to find the temperature that a particular species of fish requires. Water temperature is probably the most important determinant of the location of fish in a particular body of water or whether or not certain species are there at all.

Sophisticated Navigational Aids

The Loran-C receiver is a navigational instrument that is utilized to locate specific fishing locations. The Loran-C receiver can also help you return to the same spot later. Another precise navigation aid, known as the Global Positioning System (GPS), is very popular among anglers.

You will be more successful in your angling if you learn to locate fish, and the more you know about the species you are seeking, the more successful you will be. Maps, charts, and electronic fishing aids can also be powerful tools as you fish.

ACTIVITIES

Activity 1—How You Can See The Bottom

Since you can't see the bottom of the pond or lake you want to fish, and you may not have electronic help, how can you find those drop offs or deep holes that you would like to fish? One answer is a topographic map. Topo maps show the surface configuration of the area before the land was flooded to make the lake. They also show high spots and low spots and the slope of the ground between. Topo maps can be very important additions to your fishing equipment. Your County Agricultural Agent, school science dept., university geology dept., or public library can help you in obtaining these inexpensive maps. Secure one or more of these maps and identify areas that would be good fishing areas for different species of fish.

Activity 2—Making A Map

Making a topographical map of your fishing area can aid your understanding of the processes and forces taking place in the aquatic environment. In turn, an understanding of these will help you locate and catch fish. In the summer make a rough drawing of your fishing area in a manmade reservoir, including the slope of the banks, vegetation types and visible structures in the water. Visit the same area during the winter when the water is likely to be several feet lower and do your mapping again. Make notations of the many objects that can't be seen during the summer, but now are clearly visible. When you return the next fishing season, you will know exactly where to cast your lure. Taking pictures of these areas with your camera can be of great assistance to you as you do your mapping.

CHAPTER **6**

FISHING FROM SHORE

SHORE FISHING ADVANTAGES

Shore fishing is possible for everyone, even large family and club groups. There's no boat to own or rent, it's low in cost, and all you need is basic fishing tackle, a fishing license when required, and a shoreline.

FISHING LOCATIONS

Many anglers fish from shore. Although some species of fish are rarely caught by shore anglers, there are plenty of other species available. For example, free-swimming ocean fish are not found close to shore and deep-dwelling lake trout are seldom caught

by shore anglers; however, many species of fish are. Bottom feeders such as carp, catfish, suckers, and walleye, and those that relate to objects in the water such as largemouth and smallmouth bass, northern pike, crappie, sunfish, and stream trout, are often caught from shore.

Lakes and Ponds

Many lakes and ponds have shoreline structure such as docks, logs, stump fields, brush and rock piles, and fallen trees. These locations, which provide shelter, shade, and protection for fish, are ideal fishing spots. However, the best locations may be remote and far from roads.

Shore Fishing

Rivers and Streams

Rivers and streams are good places to fish, especially those with structure such as islands, sand bars, rocks or rock piles, and log jams within casting distance from shore. Anglers who fish shallow rivers often combine shore fishing with shallow-water wading. Fishing from the middle of a stream lets you cast to a greater choice of places. Remember, most fish face the flow of water and wait for food to come to them.

Fishing the Surf

Surf anglers fish either from the shore or wade into the shallow water. Usually there is little visible structure, so surf fishermen must learn to "read" the water to detect shallow sloughs, pockets, tide rips, and other areas where fish may be present. Learning to "read" the water can be accomplished by asking experienced anglers, observation, and fishing experience.

Piers

Fishing piers can extend from the shore for only a few feet or as much as several hundred feet. They may be as much as 20 to 30 feet above the water. Piers let anglers get their baits and lures farther out into the water than fishing from shore would allow.

Often rock piles or other structures are built next to a pier to attract fish. Even if this structure is absent, the pier pilings attract fish. Some of the best fishing is often right under a pier.

Breakwaters and Jetties

Breakwaters and jetties are similar to piers; they too, extend into the water and offer a platform from which to fish. Most are built to protect harbor areas and boat slips from the wave action of large bodies of water. Those designed for fishing have rocks arranged so that they're flat on top. Anglers fishing breakwaters and jetties that aren't flat need special cleated shoes to help keep them from slipping.

Walkways

Walkways are specially built fishing platforms that are near or run parallel to bridges, piers, shoreline bulkheads, or similar structures. An example is a walkway along a bridge, but constructed at a lower level to keep anglers safe from auto traffic and to put them closer to the water.

Bridges

Fishing isn't always allowed from bridges because of the danger from traffic. When angling is permitted, anglers must be extremely careful.

SHORE FISHING TACKLE

In most cases, tackle for shore fishing is no different from that used in fishing from a boat under the same conditions and for the same species of fish. Light freshwater tackle is used for sunfish, small catfish, trout, smallmouth bass in streams, suckers, and small walleye. Medium tackle is used for largemouth bass, smallmouth bass, northern pike, carp, large catfish, and salmon. Heavy tackle is used for large salmon and trout, muskie, striped bass, and large carp.

Medium-to-heavy tackle is commonly

used in surf fishing. Because of currents and tides, weights are used to keep bait or lures on or near the bottom. Surf fishing anglers often use a large spinning reel with 12- to 20-pound-test line and an 8- to 12-foot, heavy rod so that long casts can be made. Surf anglers usually fish with some type of bait unless fish are visible; then lures are often used.

Surf anglers also need sand spikes to hold rods upright on the shore, while wading surf fishermen need a surf belt to hold a small landing gaff, stringer, lure bag, a flashlight, and extra line.

Pier fishing tackle is slightly heavier than most shore fishing tackle because of the need to make long casts and to control a hooked fish until it can be landed. Pier anglers often use a small cart to hold extra rods and rod holders, tackle boxes, and bait containers.

APPROACHING FISH

Fish are especially wary in shallow water near shore. Anglers must walk carefully because vibrations from their footsteps can be transmitted to the water and sensed by fish, spooking them away.

Vibration is less of a problem when fishing rivers and streams because the water's current conceals most bank vibrations. Wading anglers, however, must avoid dislodging rocks that scare fish. Vibration isn't a problem when fishing from breakwaters, jetties, and piers.

When fishing still waters, an angler close to the shore must also avoid being seen by fish. Fish near the water's surface can see through the surface by a "window" that shows them a part of the shoreline.

Anglers need to keep a low profile, stay close to shrubbery, and wear dark or camouflaged clothing.

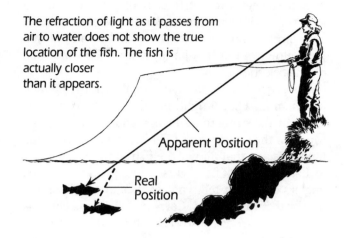

The refraction of light as it passes from air to water does not show the true location of the fish. The fish is actually closer than it appears.

Apparent Position

Real Position

HOOKING AND LANDING FISH

Setting the Hook

"Setting the hook" refers to hooking a fish. In most cases, only one sharp snap of the rod is needed to hook a fish. Some situations, however, require more force than others. For example, a single hard set is needed when using a soft-plastic worm rigged Texas style (the hook is concealed inside the worm), because the set must first drive the hook through the worm and then into the fish's mouth. Setting the hook too hard or repeatedly with a soft-mouthed fish such as a crappie, shad, or sea trout can pull the hook through the mouth.

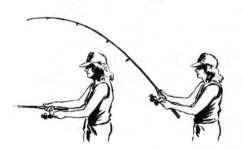

Setting The Hook

In flyfishing, anglers sometimes make a short, sharp pull with their line hand to set the hook. Others quickly raise the rod up and back to do the same thing. Many do both simultaneously to ensure that the hook secures firmly. Too much force, however, can break the line or leader or bend the hook.

Fighting a Fish

When a fish is hooked, it usually resists being reeled in and struggles to get free. It may jump, make a long run, swim back into cover or into obstructions, or swim around obstacles. Fish hooked and played in shallow water often jump, while deep-water fish often seek the bottom.

It's possible to land many small fish just by reeling them in. They'll fight, but this can be overcome easily by the strength of the line and the fishing rod. Much of the enjoyment of fishing is gained by using lighter tackle that allows the fish to fight.

Each species of fish fights differently. Experienced anglers can often tell what species of fish is on the line by the way it fights. Carp, bonefish, and chinook salmon are strong, powerful fish that tend to make long runs. Largemouth bass and steelhead trout both run and jump. Tuna dive for the bottom. Trout and tarpon fight wildly when first hooked. Northern pike and cobia (ling) often come in easily, but fight strongly near the shore or boat. Whitefish swim in a circle as they are retrieved.

Fighting larger fish requires a technique called **pumping the rod**. This is a way to retrieve line and land a strong fish whose weight is equal to or greater than the pound-test of the line. To do this, you retrieve line quickly as the rod is lowered and pointed at the fish. Then, stop retrieving line and slowly pull the rod up. When the rod is at about the 11 o'clock position, repeat the process until the fish is near and ready to be landed.

Landing a jumping fish is a problem, but it is fun. Some experienced anglers hold their rod tip underwater to keep the line down or immediately lower the rod so the line is at a low angle and is not pulling the fish up. It is important to never let the line go slack. Most jumping fish are lost when a heavy lure such as a spoon, plug, or jig is used.

Pumping The Rod

These lures wear a hole in a fish's mouth as it shakes its head. This lets it throw the lure if there is slack in the line.

Landing a Fish

Fish can be landed by hand or with tools made for that purpose. Size makes a big difference in landing any fish. Small species such as sunfish, small bass and catfish, croaker, spots, snappers, trout and others can usually be landed by raising the fish out of the water with the rod. You must, however, use care when doing this with soft-mouthed fish or when using light-wire hooks or line.

When ready to land a large fish, it is wise to slightly loosen the reel's drag because a sudden run could break the line. For this reason, tire out the fish to make landing easier. (Fish that are to be released should not be exhausted completely because it makes their recovery far more difficult.)

Nets. Landing nets are used to land fish. For boat or shore fishing, long-handled nets are used, while short-handled nets are used for stream fishing. The size of the net should match the size of fish you plan to catch.

To net a fish, lead it into the net head first. If the fish tries to escape, it will swim into the net. Once the fish is in the net, raise the net by the handle. With heavy fish also grasp the net's rim to keep the handle from bending or breaking.

Gaffs. A gaff is a large hook with a long handle. It's used to land fish that are large and difficult to net. Position the gaff so its hook enters large fish just off center of its body; smaller fish can be gaffed anywhere.

Except for those fish that are gaffed in the lip to remove a hook, lure, or fly—like big tarpon—gaffs should only be used if the fish is to be kept for food or a trophy. Fish gaffed in the body will die.

Using Your Hands. To land a fish by hand, grab it by the body (under the belly) or by the tail (for those species like chinook salmon with a strong tail that will not collapse as it is lifted).

Many anglers land bass by hand. They use their thumb and index finger to grip the fish by its lower jaw, bending their wrist back and being careful to avoid hooks. Holding a bass in this way paralyzes it temporarily and makes it easier to remove a hook or lure.

Beaching. Beaching is a popular way to land fish from shore. This method, however, should only be used if you plan to keep and eat the fish because it will harm the coating on its body. To beach a fish, lead it into increasingly shallow water, gradually sliding the fish on its side onto dry land.

Special Equipment. Bridge nets or bridge gaffs are used to land fish from bridges, jetties, and piers that are too high for an ordinary net or gaff. They are tied to a rope and lowered to the water, submerged, and raised, either to net or hook the fish.

OTHER CONSIDERATIONS

Safety

Fishing from shore isn't dangerous, but safe fishing requires common sense. In addition to following safety precautions in the "Fishing Safely" chapter, there are a few other things you need to be aware of.

- Wear footwear to protect you from glass and sharp objects.
- If you wade or fish around deep or fast moving water, use a wading stick and wear a personal flotation device (PFD).
- If fishing from a bank, beware of undercuts and unstable soil to avoid falling into the water.
- Watch for rising water levels below dams or during incoming tides. Rapidly rising water can trap you away from shore.

- Rocks, muddy banks, and fallen trees can be slick or turn, causing you to fall and suffer an injury.
- When fishing an area where there are lots of people, be particularly careful when casting. You want to catch fish, not other anglers.

Get Permission

Although many shore fishing locations are for public use, others are not. Always get permission to fish on private property and pay attention to any special requests or regulations of the landowner. Make sure all gates are left as you found them, either open or closed. Do not walk through crops or livestock. Help to keep the location clean and offer to share your catch with the landowner.

ACTIVITIES

Activity 1—Experiencing Refraction

Materials: Penny, tea cup and water.

Place the penny in the cup. Now, looking over the edge, move the cup until you can no longer see the penny. Without moving the cup, your eye or the penny, have someone pour water into the cup very slowly. Can you see the penny now? Is it really where it seems to be? What if this were a fish? The water causes the light to bend. This is called REFRACTION. Fish are not always where they appear to be.

Activity 2—Learning About Fish Senses

Much fishing is done from the shore, and it might be a good idea to consider some precautions to enhance your chances of catching fish.

How quiet should you be? Can the fish see you? Can the fish hear you? These are questions you should ask yourself as you prepare for bank fishing. To help with the answers to these questions, take a few minutes and try this:

Find a comfortable place to sit near the edge of your favorite fishing hole. Sit quietly and observe any small fish which approach in the shallows. Without moving, shout at the fish. Were they disturbed in any way? Now stomp your foot or move suddenly. How about those fish now? Try again, but this time just let your shadow fall on or near the fish. What results do you see?

Fish don't pick up sound waves from the air, so talking shouldn't bother them, but they can certainly see and pick up vibrations from the ground, so movement must be kept to a minimum. It is a good idea to know where the sun is located to avoid spooking fish with your shadow.

Activity 3—Finding Places to Fish

Do some research on places to fish near your home. Using index cards, list (1) the name of the park, river, stream, etc., (2) directions on how to reach this location, (3) any special fishing restrictions for each location, (4) types of fish that can be caught, (5) any other information you think important.

If the location is on private property, under #1 list the name, address, and phone number of the owner. Visit with each owner to determine if you would be permitted to fish on the property. Remember to ask permission prior to each fishing trip so the owner knows when you are coming.

CHAPTER 7

FISHING FROM BOATS

More water can be covered when you are fishing from a boat than from shore. In a boat you can carry extra rods, reels, and tackle boxes, a greater variety of bait, lures, and extra clothing, and use electronic equipment, such as a depthfinder, to help locate fish.

If you decide to try fishing from a boat, you need to know about:

- The boat and how it handles.
- The equipment on the boat and how it works.
- The waters you will be boating on and any hazards such as submerged trees and rocks.
- The weather conditions and emergency procedures.
- U.S. Coast Guard and state regulations.

The operator of a boat is legally responsible for the boat and the safety of those on board. The operator must also understand the rules of navigation and the courtesies of safe boating.

TYPES OF BOATS

Different types of boats are made for rivers and streams, for small lakes, or for large bodies of water. Some fishing boats are designed for special purposes, such as bass boats or large, deep-sea fishing vessels. Boats are made of many materials, including wood, fiberglass, aluminum, rubber, or other materials, and can be powered by oars or paddles and electric, gasoline, or diesel motors.

Canoes

Canoes are ideal for fishing streams, rivers and small lakes. Most canoes range from 15 to 18 feet long. They are best suited for exploring fishing waters quietly and thoroughly, but not for fishing on large bodies of water where a sudden change in weather could cause high waves.

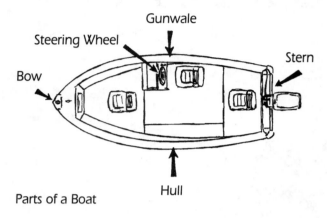

Parts of a Boat

Skiffs

The word "skiff" is often used to describe any small boat with a pointed bow, blunt stern (transom) and a flat or slightly rounded hull (boat body). They are also commonly called "rowboats," and are either rowed or powered by small outboard motors. Most skiffs are 12 to 16 feet long and are used for fishing small lakes, streams, and rivers. Skiffs are roomy and inexpensive.

Jonboats

Jonboats have a blunt bow and a flat bottom, are roomy, stable, and ideal for fishing small lakes, streams, and rivers. They are usually made of light-weight aluminum and can be carried by one or more people. Jonboats range from 8 to 20 feet long.

V-Hull Boats

V-hull boats have a "V" shaped bow that is designed to cut through rough water. V-hull boats range in length from about 15 feet to more than 40 feet. Depending on their size, they can be used on different kinds of waters. The largest can be used on very large lakes and even in the ocean.

V-hull boats have a planing hull designed to run on top of the water on a small part of the hull forward from the transom. Because the design is less

stable when at rest or at slow speeds, V-hull boats are not as comfortable for drift or anchored fishing in rough water.

Cathedral-hull Boats

The cathedral-hull boat has two or three hull sections underwater. It gets it name because, if observed out of the water, you can see an arching cathedral opening. They are wide, smooth-riding, and are stable at rest or at slow speeds. They are ideal for drift or anchored fishing in rough water.

Specialty Boats

Some boats are designed for certain kinds of fishing. These include the bass boat, which has a V-shaped bow, a large outboard motor, an electric motor, elevated seats, a live well, and plenty of storage space for tackle. They range in length from 15 to 20 feet. Although designed for bass fishing, they are also ideal for other freshwater angling and some light-tackle, near-shore saltwater fishing.

Drift boats are another popular specialty boat. Drift boats have a high bow and stern and are used to float rivers. Other specialty boats include small, light, one or two person boats for fishing ponds, inflatable rubber boats, and boats that fold for storage on a car or in another vehicle.

BOAT PROPULSION—WAYS TO MOVE BOATS

Poles, Paddles, and Oars

Long poles can be used to move small boats in shallow water. Paddles are mainly used with a canoe, but many states require that a paddle or pair of oars be part of a boat's emergency equipment. Oars can be used to move a boat on small bodies of water.

Electric Motor

A battery-powered electric motor can be used to move a boat slowly on ponds or lakes. An electric motor is often used on boats with outboard motors to control the position of the boat while fishing.

Outboard Engine

An outboard is a gasoline engine, from one-horsepower up to 300, mounted on the boat's stern (the rear of the boat). Small outboards are controlled with a steering handle, often called a "tiller," while large outboards are controlled by a steering wheel.

Inboard Engine

An inboard is a gasoline or diesel fueled engine that is installed completely inside a boat. Inboard engines are usually found on boats 18 feet or more in length. Larger boats may have two inboard engines operated by a dual control system.

Most inboards are equipped with a propeller, but in certain areas jet drives are popular. Propellers provide more efficient performance than jets. However, jet drives allow boats into shallower and rockier areas than boats with propellers.

Inboard/Outboard

An inboard/outboard, commonly called an "I/O," or stern drive, combines some features of the outboard and inboard engines. An I/O's engine is mounted inside the boat in front of the transom. Its power goes through the stern of the boat and into an outboard-like lower unit to the propeller.

Anchoring, Mooring, and Docking

Anchors. There are many types and sizes of anchors for different sizes of boats. It is important that a boat have the proper anchor and an anchor line about 10 times the depth of water in which it will be anchored.

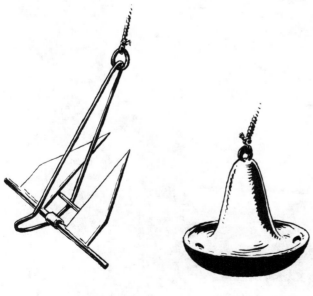

Danforth Anchor   Mushroom Anchor

Some anchor types and their uses include:

- **Danforth Anchor.** This anchor has two flat metal flukes that dig into the bottom. The Danforth anchor is light for its size and holding ability and works best in most hard, but not rocky, bottoms.
- **Mushroom Anchor.** This anchor looks like an upside-down mushroom and holds small boats in waters with sandy or muddy bottoms. It has less holding power than a Danforth and doesn't hold well on hard, marl, or rocky bottoms.

Docking and Mooring. Docking and mooring a boat is not difficult, but requires skill and practice.

In calm water, control the boat's movement with the motor to carefully position the boat at the dock. When docking in a current or waves, for maximum control, take the boat into a dock by heading it into the current. If this isn't possible, keep the motor in reverse and let the boat drift slowly to the dock.

When mooring a boat, both stern and bow lines must be used. For permanent docking, "spring lines" must also be used to hold the boat properly inside the boat slip to prevent it from rubbing against the dock or pilings and to allow for changes in water levels.

Navigation and Navigation Aids

Navigation involves finding the way from one point to another. Navigation is often done visually, but other methods include the use of navigation charts, compass headings, or electronic equipment, like a Global Positioning System.

For navigating with a chart and compass heading, a boat must have a properly adjusted compass. Learn to use a compass correctly, and always carry one on board in the event you lose visibility due to fog, rain, or darkness. The boater must have basic navigation skills, such as knowing how to read a chart and run time-distance courses. These skills allow the boat to be placed at a certain location based on the boat's speed and the time taken to get there.

The Loran-C receiver is an instrument that receives signals from land-based stations. It allows a boater to locate an exact spot on the water in all kinds of weather, even in fog. Loran-C is an important safety device on large bodies of water and is also useful for finding favorite fishing locations.

Another even more precise navigation aid for boaters and others is the Global Positioning System (GPS). GPS uses signals from several orbiting satellites to determine a precise position-often within 30 feet-on the water, on land, or in the air.

NAVIGATION SYMBOLS

Uniform waterway markers help boaters navigate by warning them of dangerous areas and helping locate channels. It is the responsibility of all boaters to understand the meaning of navigation buoys and that they should never moor to one.

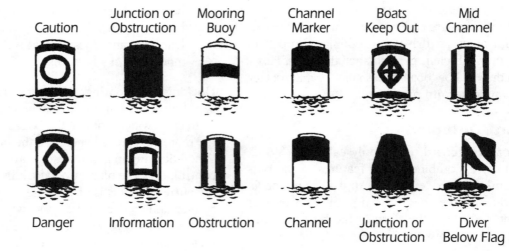

Caution   Junction or Obstruction   Mooring Buoy   Channel Marker   Boats Keep Out   Mid Channel

Danger   Information   Obstruction   Channel   Junction or Obstruction   Diver Below Flag

Shoal

FLOAT PLAN

Always let someone know your boating plan and when you will return. This can save your life in an emergency.

BOATING LAWS

Anglers using boats must obey boating laws. A boat must have emergency equipment on board. For example, a *U.S. Coast Guard-approved personal flotation device (PFD) is required for each person on board*. Other equipment depends on the type and length of the boat. For safe boating you should:

- **Successfully complete a boating safety course.**
- **Wear PFD's.**
- **Refrain from using alcohol while operating a boat.**
- **Watch your boat's wake. Your are responsible for damage caused by the wake.**
- **Drive at a safe speed.**
- **Stay outside of protected or swimming areas.**
- **Stay clear of swimmers and anglers.**
- **Avoid the path of other boats.**
- **Remain seated in small boats. In large boats, remain seated while boat is moving. Always wear your PFD.**
- **Anchor outside of shipping channels.**
- **Never overload boats with passengers or equipment.**
- **Use navigation lights at night.**
- **Use the right-size motor.**

Boaters must follow the **Rules of the Road**, which include knowing which boat has the right-of-way. Sailboats have the right-of-way over powerboats. U.S. Navigation Rules include:

- **Boats approaching each other must stay to the right at all times and pass each other port (left) side to port side.**
- **Yield the right of way to other boats being overtaken. You can overtake another boat on either side, but you must use caution so that your boat's wake does not endanger the boat being passed.**
- **When boats approach at an angle, the boat on the starboard (right) side has the right of way and must hold its course and speed. The other boat must stay clear and pass behind the boat with the right of way.**

STORMS

Boating during storms can be dangerous, especially when there is lightning, strong wind, or high waves. However, if you get caught, make sure everyone is wearing a PFD and put all fishing rods in the bottom of the boat. Stay low and lie down in the boat to reduce the risk of capsizing. Get off the water as soon as you can.

If you can't get off the water, try to prevent waves from coming in over the stern or striking the boat on its side. The best way is to keep the boat moving at a slight angle into the waves. Moving with the waves can be dangerous, because waves can come over the transom, swamping the boat.

If you must ride out a storm on the water, use a heavy anchor with a long rope attached to the bow. To be effective, the anchor line needs to be at least 10 times the depth of the water so that the anchor can hold to the bottom. If the anchor drags, make sure that the boat is not pulled into rocks, or shallow, or rougher water.

Don't fish during an electrical storm. Anglers are killed every year when their rods or boats are hit by lightning.

EMERGENCIES

By staying alert and watching out for other people and potentially hazardous situations, conditions causing boats to sink or capsize can be avoided. Many accidents are caused by speeding, unsafe turns, overloaded boats, or hitting underwater objects. Capsizing and people falling overboard cause many life-threatening situations. Everyone should wear a PFD at all times.

If someone falls overboard, throw a PFD with a line attached. Then, carefully bring the boat to the person and stop the engine.

Every boat with a gasoline motor should have at least one fire extinguisher. It should be a Coast Guard-approved extinguisher for electrical and gasoline fires. Keep it where it can be reached quickly, but not too close to the engine.

BOAT READINESS CHECKLIST

A checklist helps assure your boat is ready for use. Your checklist should include the following items:

- **Fishing Licenses.** Fishing licenses, where required, must be carried while fishing.
- **Boat Registration.** Boat registrations, when required, must be carried while using a boat.
- **Fuel.** The fuel tank should be filled before each trip. Use the 1/3 rule: use 1/3 of your fuel for the trip out, 1/3 for the trip back, and keep 1/3 in reserve in case of an emergency. Always clean up any spilled gasoline.
- **Fire Extinguisher.** Carry at least one Coast Guard-approved fire extinguisher.
- **Lights.** A boat used at night must have operating navigation lights, which include a red (port) light, a green (starboard) light, and a white stern or masthead light. Check to make sure they are working.
- **Personal Flotation Devices.** PFDs are required on all boats, and some boats also must have at least one PFD that can be thrown to a person in the water. Wear your PFD, making sure it fits properly. Test it in a pool or swimming area to assure that it can float you with the clothing you normally wear fishing.
- **Paddle or Oars.** Because motors tend to break down at the worst times, oars or a paddle are an absolute must for emergency use.
- **Lines.** Lines (ropes) are not legally required, but are necessary for docking, anchoring, mooring, or towing.
- **Other Items.** Other items that may be included in a **BOATER'S DUFFEL BAG** are:

  Spotlight
  VHF Radio
  Lake Map
  Chart and Compass
  Rope
  Visual Distress Signals

Bailer (can, scoop, bucket)
Binoculars
Food and Water
Medical Supplies
   First Aid Kit
   Special Medications
   Sunblock (SPF 15, at least)
Tool Kit
Flares
Whistle or Horn
Sunglasses
Extra Clothing
   Sun Hat
   Rain Gear
   Wool Sweater
   Stocking Cap
   Gloves

The Coast Guard Auxiliary, the United States Power Squadron, and some state agencies offer courtesy boat examinations to see that a boat has the required safety equipment on board.

METHODS OF BOAT FISHING

Still Fishing

Still fishing from an anchored boat is especially effective for bluegill, crappie and other panfish. Slip bobbers are very popular for still fishing because they allow anglers to present baits at the same depth as the fish. Slip bobbers make it easier to cast baits to desired locations. There is less line below the bobber and there is less chance of hooking another angler in the boat.

Baits should be fished with the least possible weight so that they appear as the fish's natural food.

Casting

Casting is a necessary skill to increase fishing success. Casting from a boat is a favorite method of fishing for bass and many other species. Anglers use trolling motors to position the boat near the shore, structure, weedbeds, or other cover. They then cast their lure or bait to locations where fish may be. After several casts the boat is moved to another nearby location.

Proper presentation of the lure or bait is important to fishing success. Many anglers recommend that the lure or bait be cast beyond the point where the fish is expected to be. The lure is then retrieved past the location of the fish.

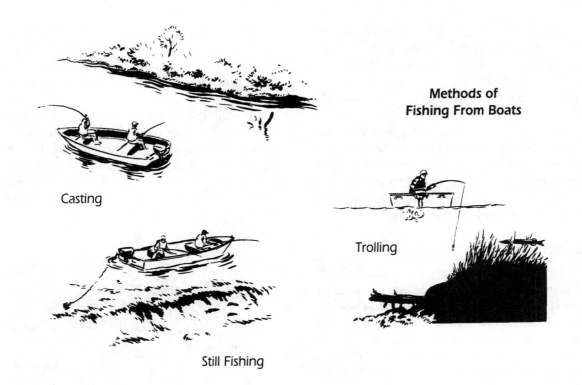

Casting

Still Fishing

Methods of Fishing From Boats

Trolling

Varying the retrieve of the lure or bait is also important. Fish strike when the presentation appears to be natural and when there is erratic movement. Techniques that vary the motion, speed, and movement of the lure increase fishing success. Twitches, pauses, jerks, short constant retrieves or repeated jerks are often successful. You will learn which techniques work for different species as you gain fishing experience.

Trolling

Trolling is allowing a lure to trail behind a moving boat. It can be used for any fish that will strike a lure in either fresh or salt water. Trolling is an excellent way to quickly explore an area for fish. Successful anglers vary their speed and direction, and experiment using lures of different colors. When the experimentation locates fish and the lures they are striking, more fish can be caught. Usually, lures or baits are run straight off of a rod. However, side planers, downriggers, outriggers, motor plates, kites and other gear are used for certain species of fish and types of water.

Drifting

Drift fishing is similar to still fishing, but the boat is not anchored. While drift fishing, boats turn sideways against the wind. The wind pushes the boat across the water while anglers drift their baits. Drift fishing is a successful technique for many species of fish.

BOAT MAINTENANCE

Boats and related equipment must be properly maintained and stored. Proper maintenance includes a careful inspection of the boat, ideally after each trip. The hull, engine, and accessories, such as navigation lights, should be checked to see if they are operating properly. Other equipment should be examined for wear or damage.

Engines come with an owner's manual containing maintenance and lubrication schedules. These should be followed carefully. A log also should be kept to record the hours of use because engine maintenance is based on hours of operation. Of particular importance is the change of lower unit lubrication or grease on outboards and I/Os because lack of lubrication can quickly damage an engine.

TRAILERING A BOAT

Trailering a boat is an important skill. It requires a trailer designed for the boat's length and weight and with rollers or slide pads. A good trailer hitch, safety chains, and lighting connection are required on all trailers.

Check to be sure the tail lights and turn signals work when attached to the towing vehicle. Make sure the outboard or out-drive is raised to clear obstacles. When rounding sharp turns, remember to swing wide to keep from cutting the corner with the trailer.

Before attempting your first launch, tow your boat to an empty parking lot and practice backing your trailer. If you want the rear of the trailer to go right, turn the steering wheel left. If it is to go left, turn the steering wheel right. When backing, it is a good idea to have a lookout help direct you.

Launching A Boat

Because boat ramps are usually busy places and to avoid making others wait, remember to use common courtesy. Prepare your boat for launching before you get to the boat ramp. Load the boat with all fishing tackle, boating gear, and personal flotation devices (PFDs). The boat tie-down straps must be removed, the trailer's tail light connection disconnected, the engine raised, and the line attached to the boat held by someone on shore or the dock. Double check the drain plug to be sure it is in place.

Many trailers allow the boat to be driven on and off. If yours does not, attach a line to the boat's bow and have another person hold on to the end to keep the boat from drifting.

Once the boat is launched, immediately drive the vehicle and trailer off the ramp while another member of your party pulls the boat to shore or toward the dock for boarding.

Loading

Check the capacity plate located on your boat. Do not overload by taking on too many passengers or too much equipment.

Step in—don't jump in—your boat and have passengers come aboard one at a time. Place passengers so the boat is evenly balanced front to rear and side to side. Weight distributed unevenly will affect the boat's performance.

Have someone on the dock hand you any gear. Distribute it evenly and, if possible, stow it out of the way. PFD's should be worn and other life-saving gear placed where it can be reached quickly. Place gasoline containers in the stern and clamped in brackets or held down with cords. Anchors should be stored in the bow with the anchor line coiled neatly for instant use.

Store batteries in battery boxes with terminals covered to prevent electrical shorting and fires. Store all other gear, including fishing tackle, so that it doesn't move around or blow out when the boat is moving.

Sit while the boat is underway. Never sit on the top of seat backs or on the deck or gunwales. Doing so is unsafe and illegal. If you are sitting in or fishing from the bow of an open-bow boat, be especially careful. If the boat hits a submerged object or even a wave or the wake of another boat, you could be thrown out.

DON'T SPREAD NUISANCE SPECIES

Remove all weeds from your boat and trailer before launching. Weeds, such as milfoil, can be spread from lake to lake by boaters. Milfoil can ruin fishing by spreading rapidly and interfering with boating access. Excess vegetation can also protect too many small fish, causing an overpopulation. In addition, when these weeds die, they decompose, creating low oxygen conditions that can cause fish to die.

A notorious example of the unintentional introduction of a "nuisance species" is the zebra mussel which was transferred to the Great Lakes through ship ballast water and has become a threat to biological diversity in affected waters. This mollusk, which proliferates rapidly, fouls boat hulls and engines, dock and marina pilings, navigation buoys, and municipal and power plant water intakes, is a perfect example of the unintended introduction of a nuisance species.

COURTESY ON THE WATER

Common sense and courtesy make everyone's day on the water safer and more enjoyable. People go boating to have fun and more fun will occur if everyone's rights are respected and all rules of boat and water safety are followed.

ACTIVITIES

Activity 1—Why Clean Your Boat

Big pollution problems can occur when unwanted organisms are carried from one place to another. Anglers are sometimes unwitting agents of this pollution.

Take a sprig of seaweed from your local fishing spot. Allow it to dry for a day or two and then put it into a bucket of water. Examine it after a couple of days. Notice that it is alive and well. Scrape some scum off the hull of your boat and do the same thing. Also check for nuisance species such as zebra mussels.

Did you ever wonder how ponds become home to these organisms? How might you cut down on this problem?

Activity 2—Safety Checklist

Develop a safety checklist for your boat and have it laminated or covered with plastic. This list should be left in the boat as a reminder to you before you leave shore. Also, it would be available for friends if you loan them your boat.

Activity 3—Comparing Boat Features

Visit a local marina or boat shop and examine the hulls of the available boats. There is a wide range of bow shapes which determine the handling of a boat in the water. Which shape would cut through the water easily and thus provide speed? Which would provide the most maneuverability? Which type has the largest bottom surface area and would provide stability? If you are contemplating the purchase of a boat or even renting one, keep in mind how shape and surface area influence the boat's function.

CHAPTER 8

CARING FOR YOUR CATCH

A fish that you plan to eat must be kept fresh. To ensure its freshness it must be kept alive until it is cleaned. You can put live fish in the livewell of a boat or on a stringer in the water. If a fish can't be kept alive, it should be cleaned and placed on ice to avoid spoilage. If you don't plan to keep a fish, free it quickly without harming it.

CLEANING FISH TO EAT

Fish can be cleaned and prepared in a variety of ways. A knife is necessary in cleaning fish. Use caution because knives can be dangerous if used improperly. If you have any slime on your hands or on the knife handle, wash it off to prevent slipping. Always keep your hands in back of the blade. For added safety, wear metal-mesh "fish-cleaning" gloves to protect your hands.

One way to clean fish is to remove the entrails. First, insert the knife tip into the fish's vent and move the blade up along the belly, cutting to the head. Keep the knife blade shallow so you don't puncture the intestines. Then, spread the body open and remove all of the entrails. Some fish have a kidney by the backbone. You can remove it by scraping it out with a spoon or your thumbnail. Cut off the head and rinse the fish in clean water.

To keep a dressed fish fresh, surround it with ice in a chest or cooler. As the ice melts, the water should drain from the cooler because it spoils the flavor of fish.

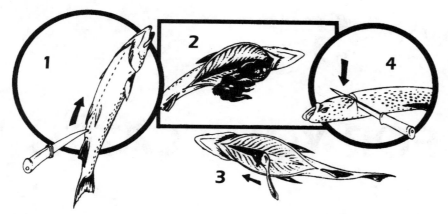

Cleaning a Fish

To skin a catfish or bullhead, hold its head firmly with a clamp. For safety, it is a good idea to snip off a catfish's spines before skinning. Then, cut through the skin behind the head and the pectoral fins. Use pliers to remove the skin from the body, pulling from the head toward the tail. Grasp the head of the fish with one hand and the body with the other. Break the backbone at the head. Pull the head and entrails away from the skinned body. After you wash the fish in clean water, it's ready for cooking. You remove the fish's bones just before you eat it.

People also fillet catfish. However, they are more difficult to fillet than most other fish.

Filleting. Filleting means getting the meat of the fish without the bones. Larger fish, such as largemouth bass, northern pike, salmon, and walleye, are usually filleted. A filleted fish has its skin and all of its bones removed before cooking. Scaling isn't necessary.

Fillet knives have a long, thin, blade that is very sharp and specifically designed for filleting fish. A fillet knife is dangerous and must be handled safely.

To fillet a fish, lay it on its side on a flat surface. Cut the fish behind its gills and pectoral fin down to, but not through, the backbone. Without removing the knife, turn the blade and cut through the ribs toward the tail. Use the fish's backbone to guide you. Turn the fish over and repeat the steps.

Most saltwater fish don't keep well when put in a livewell or kept on a stringer. They must be put on ice to insure freshness.

Scaling a Fish

Scaling. Scaling means to remove the scales from the skin of a fish. Scale fish on a flat surface, using one hand to hold it by the head. Rake the scales from the tail toward the head with a fish scaler or a large spoon. Remove the scales on both sides of the body. After you remove the head, gills, entrails, and fins, the fish can be cooked with its skin on. Small fish, like bluegill and crappie, are usually scaled, cleaned, and then cooked whole. Cook scaled fish with the bones in the body, and remove them just before you eat.

Skinning. Removing the skin improves the taste of many fish. It also removes a layer of fat just under the skin. Catfish are usually skinned.

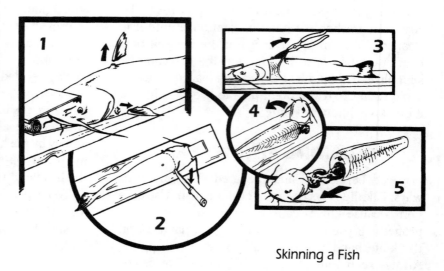

Skinning a Fish

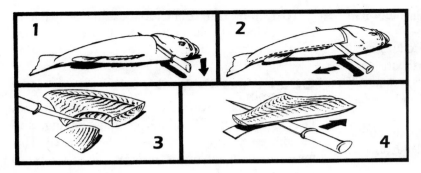

Filleting a Fish

Next, insert the knife blade close to the rib bones and slice the entire rib section of each fillet away. Then, with the skin-side down, insert the knife blade about a 1/2 inch from the tail. Gripping this tail part firmly, put the blade between the skin and the meat at an angle. Using a little pressure and a sawing motion, cut against—not through—the skin. The fillet will be removed from the skin.

Wash each fillet in cold water. Pat dry with a clean cloth or paper towel. The fillets are ready to cook or freeze.

Steaking. A large fish is often cut into thick steaks by cutting across the body. First, clean the fish and skin or scale it. Usually a fish is scaled only if the scales make it difficult to cut the steaks. Before steaking, chill the fish or put it in a freezer until it is partly stiff.

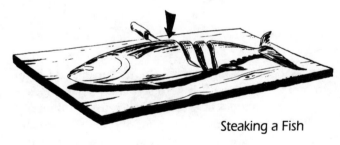

Steaking a Fish

For most fish, cut through the body, working from the tail toward the head. Make each steak from 1/2-inch to 1-inch thick. After steaking, trim away any belly fat or bones that you can see, but not the backbone.

STORING FISH

Keep fish alive or chilled from the time they are caught until stored. Clean as soon as possible to preserve the flavor. If they are iced or chilled, fish can be kept for up to a day before cleaning. There are several ways to store fish after they are prepared for cooking.

Icing. After fish are dressed, they can be iced. This is the best way to transport them. Use an insulated cooler and leave the cooler's drain plug open so the water will run out since water spoils their flavor.

Refrigeration. Before refrigerating fish, wash in cold water and dry with a clean cloth or paper towel. Then wrap in waxed paper, plastic wrap, or aluminum foil and store on ice or in the refrigerator. Usually you can store fish in the refrigerator for up to two days. Large fish or large pieces of fish will keep longer than small pieces. Lean fish, such as panfish and walleye store better than fatty fish, like trout.

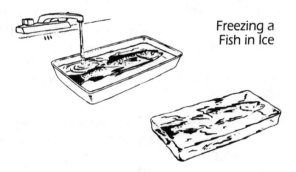

Freezing a Fish in Ice

Freezing. Frozen fish last from 3 to 12 months. However, the preparation for freezing is important. Fish can lose its flavor by coming in contact with air. One way to prevent this is to wrap fish in aluminum foil. Then, wrap again with freezer paper.

Another way to preserve flavor is to freeze fish in a solid block of ice. Place the fish into a refrigerator container and use enough water to just cover the fish.

To thaw frozen fish, put it in the refrigerator overnight or place the wrapped fish in cold water. Don't thaw fish at room temperature or in a microwave. A microwave will begin to cook part of the fish before other parts are thawed.

Other Ways. Smoking, pickling, and canning are other ways to store or prepare fish. Smoking is an excellent way to preserve and prepare fish for eating. Smoking imparts a unique flavor to fish and is a good way to prepare underutilized species such as carp.

Pickling is a method of preparing fish that uses a brine or lime solution. The freshly cleaned and chunked fish is preserved by the pickling solution in which it is stored.

Canning uses standard canning procedures and pressure cooker processing. Canned fish are used for casseroles, stews, chowders, appetizers, and salads because the fish is in chunk form and already cooked.

Look for recipes in cookbooks or your public library and from state natural resource departments.

WAYS TO COOK FISH

Frying. Many fish are panfried; however, broiling or baking are also popular methods of cooking fish. Panfrying is cooking both sides of the fish in hot cooking oil. Coat the fish with flour, breading, cornmeal, or batter before frying. The batter mix can be a pancake-type batter or one made with spices or even a little baking soda. Heat the oil in a skillet and put a small piece of fish in it. If it sizzles, the oil is hot enough.

There are many recipes for cooking fish found in most cookbooks. Here is a simple recipe for panfried fish.

Panfried Fish
Ingredients:
Lean whole fish, dressed
1/2 cup milk
1 egg
1/2 cup flour
Salt, pepper, and herb seasoning
Cooking oil, butter, or margarine
Lemon
Parsley

Mix the egg and milk. Dip the fish into the egg-milk mixture and then coat the fish with flour. Instead of flour, you can use a heavier, breaded coating or pancake batter. Turn on the burner and set it to a high heat. Put oil, butter, or margarine into the cooking pan or skillet. Use enough to cover the bottom to a depth of 1/8 to 1/4 inch. When the oil is hot, put in the fish. Adjust the heat so the oil will not smoke or burn. Cook until the fish is brown on one side, then turn it over and cook the other side. When done, remove from the pan and place on a paper towel to drain. Put the fish on a serving platter and sprinkle with lemon juice and parsley. Butter and herbs are also tasty on panfried fish.

To deep-fry fish, submerge them in a deep pan of hot cooking oil. Fillets or small fish can be used with or without batter.

Other Ways To Cook Fish

There are many ways to cook fish that are both tasty and healthy. **Broiling, grilling, baking, and poaching** are popular because oil is not used. This makes them healthier for those people who have to watch their diets.

The **microwave** is an especially good way to cook fish quickly and easily. Place fillets in a microwave dish, add a liquid like water or lemon juice, cover, and cook on high for six or seven minutes for one pound of fillets. Let stand for 5 minutes and then eat.

Broiling. Broiling uses a high-temperature heat above the fish, with the fish turned over halfway through the cooking. High heat dries out some fish, so basting with butter, cooking oil, lemon-butter, or other sauces helps to keep the fish moist and tender.

Broiling is a quick way to cook small fish or fillets. Only several minutes on each side is required.

Broiled Fish
Ingredients:
Fish fillets
Chicken broth or bouillon cubes
Lemon juice
Butter
Salt
Paprika

Coat a baking pan with butter or oil, add fish and sprinkle the fish with salt and paprika. Heat the fish under the oven's broiler for 3 minutes. Then, remove the pan, pour the chicken broth over the fish, and return the pan to the broiler for 10 to 15 minutes. Just before serving, sprinkle some lemon juice or butter over the fish.

Grilling. Cooking on a barbecue grill prepares fish quickly using high temperature. Fillets, steaks, or dressed whole fish can be grilled, but thick portions are best to keep the fish from falling apart when turned over or removed.

Place the fish on a hot grill and baste frequently. When almost done, turn over and grill the other side.

Check the fish by separating the flesh; it should be white and flaky, but not dry and brittle.

Baking. Baking is best for preparing large fish. It also helps prevent lean fish from drying out. Baking involves basting the fish with natural juices, butter, cooking oil, or sauces, and cooking in a covered pan using a moderate temperature. Cooking times for baked fish are longer than for panfried, broiled, or grilled fish.

Baked Fish

Ingredients:

Whole, steaked, filleted, or canned fish or fish chunks

1 to 2 cups sour cream, salad dressing, or thick vegetable stew

Salt and pepper

Place fish in a baking pan and cover with sour cream, salad dressing, or the stew. Add salt and pepper to taste. Cover the pan and place in a baking oven for 20 to 30 minutes at 350° F.

Poaching. Poaching is a good way to cook large fish because the flavor is preserved without drying them out. Special poaching pans—a long pan with a lid—are made for this. The whole cleaned fish, with the head usually left on, is placed on a rack that comes with the pan. The fish is covered with a light vegetable—or herb-spiced broth and cooked until done.

Simmering is much like poaching, but uses the higher temperature of a rolling boil to shorten the cooking time.

Steaming is similar to poaching, but instead of cooking the fish in a liquid, it is cooked by the steam coming from liquid under the fish.

Most poaching and steaming cooking times are about 15 minutes. To prevent poached, simmered, and steamed fish from breaking apart when removing them from the pan, wrap the fish in cheese cloth before cooking.

SAFETY OF EATING FISH

Most fish are safe to eat. However, some waters are polluted in such ways that make some fish unsafe to eat. Most often the health benefits of adding low-cholesterol fish to your diet greatly outweigh any health risks. If you are unsure of the safety of the area you are fishing, contact your state's natural resources agency or health department.

Some contaminant problems in fish can be reduced by cleaning fish carefully. Skinning fish removes fat under the skin. Since contaminants can be contained in this fat, trim fat from around the backbone, along the sides, and from the belly of the fish.

Smaller fish are generally safer than large, top-of-the-food chain predators. With larger fish, contaminants have had more time to accumulate.

ACTIVITIES

Activity 1—Cossack Asparagus

Catching fish is not the only pleasure associated with fishing. Eating what you catch is equally enjoyable. How about trying a different menu with those fresh fish? There are many edible wild plants that can be prepared and served to add spice to a fish fry. Try this one: In shallow water, find cattail shoots which are sticking up about 2 feet above the water. Pull gently and they should come loose below the water line. There will be a white area several inches long at the end. Cut this off and peel the outer layers. Boil these in salted water for 3–4 minutes. Drain and top with some butter. This is Cossack Asparagus.

There are several books that tell you how to recognize, collect and prepare edible wild plants:

Stalking the Wild Asparagus, Gibbons
Stalking the Good Life, Gibbons
Beachcomber's Handbook, Gibbons
Field Guide to Edible Wild Plants, Angier

Your local library will probably have others.

Activity 2—Making a Recipe File

Many fish markets or grocery stores that sell fresh fish have printed recipes for you to take and try. Many of the fish you catch will taste very good using one of these recipes. Adding them to your recipe collection will provide variety in your fish menu. Make copies of the good ones and encourage your friends to try them. They may give you some of their favorites in return.

Print or type these recipes on 3 x 5 index cards and store in a simple file box where they are accessible.

CHAPTER 9

FISHING ETHICS AND YOUR PERSONAL COMMITMENT

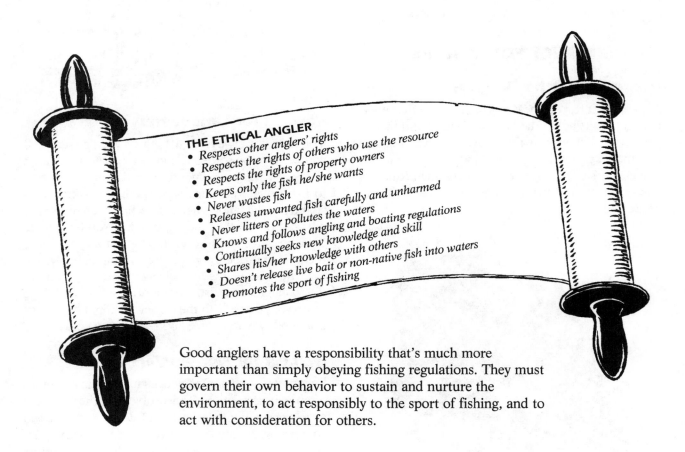

THE ETHICAL ANGLER
- Respects other anglers' rights
- Respects the rights of others who use the resource
- Respects the rights of property owners
- Keeps only the fish he/she wants
- Never wastes fish
- Releases unwanted fish carefully and unharmed
- Never litters or pollutes the waters
- Knows and follows angling and boating regulations
- Continually seeks new knowledge and skill
- Shares his/her knowledge with others
- Doesn't release live bait or non-native fish into waters
- Promotes the sport of fishing

Good anglers have a responsibility that's much more important than simply obeying fishing regulations. They must govern their own behavior to sustain and nurture the environment, to act responsibly to the sport of fishing, and to act with consideration for others.

PERSONAL FISHING RESPONSIBILITY

Protecting and Preserving Aquatic Resources

As more people discover fishing, the demands are certain to grow. It may be a demand for a specific species of fish or for larger or more fish. Other anglers may demand more fishing waters. Answering such demands becomes extremely complex and, in some cases, may be impossible.

Natural habitat is often sacrificed for housing, shopping centers, schools, and other development. In the process, aquatic resources may be lost. Pollution lowers the fish-carrying capacity of bodies of water and further diminishes the resource. The carrying capacity limits the number of fish in any body of water. Of immediate concern are measures to protect and preserve aquatic resources for future generations.

Minimize Individual Impact

The impact of one angler on the total resource might seem insignificant. Does it really make a difference how many fish an angler keeps or how the angler treats the habitat? One angler may not have a significant impact, but there is a cumulative effect. What one person does adds to the behavior and attitude of the next person and so on. The bottom line is attitude. Anglers must recognize that whatever is done has an impact on the overall picture.

RESPECT FOR OTHERS

Respect for Other Anglers

Anglers must respect the rights of others. Some people may enjoy sitting on the bank of a pond and fishing peacefully. Others may prefer using a boat. You can fish the way you like and not judge how someone else chooses to fish. Following the Golden Rule is a good plan; treat other anglers as you would like to be treated.

Crowded Anglers

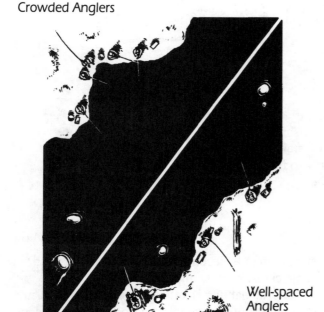

Well-spaced Anglers

For example, if you are fishing, would you like to have another angler start fishing too close to you?

You would probably be angry because the other angler was crowding you! If you moved from your spot to land a fish, you would feel that you had the right to return to your original fishing spot. When we respect the rights of others as we enjoy fishing, it makes the day more pleasant for everyone.

Respect for Landowners

You may not always be fishing on public waters. If you must cross someone's land to get to the water, always ask the landowner for permission. If you want to fish privately owned waters, always ask permission from the landowner before fishing. This is true whether or not the land is posted. If you have to go through gates, be sure to leave them as you found them. If you open a gate, close it immediately. Do not litter! Leave the area cleaner than you found it. If you catch some fish from a private pond, offer to share your catch with the owner. Doing these things is a good way to assure an invitation to come back.

Respect for Non-Anglers

Encounters with non-anglers using aquatic resources often causes friction. The problem is that non-anglers are frequently unaware of what is involved in conserving aquatic resources. Nothing bothers an angler more than a water skier disturbing prime fish habitat or the sight of hikers or campers damaging the banks of a stream. Sightseers speeding across tarpon waters in high-powered boats anger fly rod anglers stalking these fish.

The resource, however, should be shared by everyone. Angry confrontations seldom solve problems. Education can help people understand the needs of anglers and can help anglers understand other outdoor users.

RESPECT FOR THE RESOURCE

Good anglers respect our country's water resources. These resources need to be protected so that others can enjoy them. We all share this responsibility. There are many things we can do to care for our water resources.

Never Litter

Never leave any litter behind. If you walk to a fishing spot, carry out everything you carried in. This includes food wrappers, old fishing line, bait containers, empty cans or bottles, and plastic bags. Pick up litter left behind by others, too. It is easy to carry a small paper bag for this purpose. If you are fishing from a boat, be sure your litter is put into a closed container so it can't blow out. If we all do these things, our lakes and streams will be much cleaner.

Picking Up Litter

Sinking empty soda cans or bottles is no better than leaving them on shore. You are littering the bottom of the lake. Carry empty containers when you leave your fishing spot and recycle them.

Never Waste Fish

Good anglers know that fish are food and shouldn't be wasted. Keep only the number of fish that you can use; release others quickly and carefully. If you want to show your fish to others, take a picture before releasing it. The picture will bring you many fond memories, and the fish can bring enjoyment to another angler.

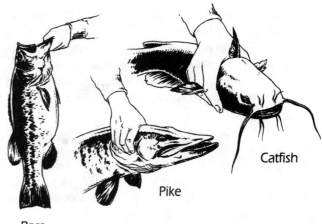

Catfish

Pike

Bass

How To Hold Fish

Releasing A Fish

To release a fish, keep it in the water if you can. Handle it carefully with a wet hand or wet towel so it can be freed unharmed. If it's a fish without sharp teeth like a bass, hold its lower lip between your thumb and index finger. If it has sharp teeth like a walleye or northern pike, carefully hold it around the body. Never hold a fish by the eyes or gills if it is to be released.

Tearing a hook out can harm a fish so badly that it may not live. If the fish is hooked deeply and the hook can't easily be removed, cut the line to release the fish. The hook will rust, dissolve, or become loose without causing harm. The use of barbless hooks also makes it easy to release fish.

If a fish loses consciousness, try to revive it by **gently** moving it in a figure-eight pattern so water passes through its gills. When the fish begins to struggle and can swim, let it go.

Today, some species of fish exist in limited numbers. More and more anglers know this and participate in "catch and release" fishing. Now, many

CATCH AND RELEASE ONLY!

anglers take only what they need for food and release the rest unharmed. This makes it possible for other anglers to enjoy catching them again.

In some fisheries, catch and release is mandatory. Many "blue-ribbon" trout streams and tarpon fisheries are managed as strictly catch-and-release areas.

Some fish take longer to become adults and may not spawn (lay their eggs) until they are three to seven years old. Since they spawn only once a year, we should release as many of these fish as possible. They include bass, lake trout, muskellunge, northern pike, sturgeon, walleye, and most large game fish. Catching and then releasing these species is a good practice.

Other fish species mature earlier and spawn more than once a year. For example, bluegill and many other panfish spawn when they are two to three years old.

Until recently, few anglers realized that the populations of certain game fish in the large oceans could become threatened. Today, redfish, snook, seatrout, striped bass, and other saltwater fish, are being raised for stocking. However, hatcheries are only a part of a successful fishery management program and should not be viewed as a substitute for good management of fish populations and habitat.

ANGLER INVOLVEMENT

Know and Follow Fishing Regulations

Fishing laws are meant to protect the resource and make sure there is fishing to be shared by everyone. If you fish, it's important that you know and follow the rules and regulations. Ignorance of the law is no excuse. Fishing is a wonderful privilege; obeying fishing regulations is the responsibility that goes with it.

If there are fishing seasons, you must know them. Seasons protect fish during spawning and limit the catch on heavily fished waters. Limits on the number of fish that can be caught are meant to keep anglers from taking too many fish at one time. This makes it possible for more people to share the resource.

Report Violators

Anglers also have a responsibility to help state agencies protect our natural resources. Today, many states have a special telephone number so individuals can report those who violate fish and game laws.

Protect the Area Around the Waters

Protect the beauty of nature. Do not spray paint or carve names or other words on rocks or trees. Do not drive through streams and riparian areas. Do not destroy or pick wildflowers and other plants growing in the wild; leave them for other people to enjoy.

Continually Seek New Knowledge and Skill

A good angler is always trying to learn more—increasing fishing skills, learning more about the behavior of fish, and learning more about protecting the resource. In this way, you become part of the solution, not part of the problem. You don't have to know it all now; something new can be learned on each fishing trip.

Donating money to a good cause is one way of helping, but there's no substitute for contributing your time to help protect our natural resources. Each angler must decide what he or she is willing to do and then volunteer.

Each angler has a responsibility to become well-informed on current issues affecting the sport and the aquatic resources that make it possible. Read newspapers, magazines, and books, and listen to radio and television programs that report on such issues. Good anglers then share their knowledge with others and introduce their friends to the sport of fishing and the benefits of protecting the environment.

Participate In Resource Enhancement Projects

A good angler gets involved in projects to enhance the resource. Some students do it as a class project.

Others join or form clubs or other organizations whose members will work on projects such as improving a stretch of water on a stream, building fish structure in lakes, or cleaning up the bank around a lake, stream, or river. Besides helping improve the resource, such activities provide a good example for others to follow.

Don't let someone else worry about our natural resources. Every user must share part of the responsibility, and there are many ways you can help.

Legislative Actions

Many elected officials are not well-versed on environmental issues, so this is an area where anglers can do some good. Anglers know what is happening to their local waters. Making their views known to those who develop and vote on legislation is vital. Contact with legislators should be meaningful. Letters stating your views should be short, to the point, and deal strictly with the issue.

WHY FISHING IS A GOOD ENVIRONMENTAL SPORT AND RECREATION

There's no sport like fishing. It has universal appeal and is not limited by age, sex, race, education, physical ability or financial means. Anyone can fish and have fun doing it.

There's no better way to learn about the outdoors than to be a part of it through fishing. Anglers have an excellent opportunity to observe all types of wildlife, to appreciate the outdoors and to help sustain it for future generations.

ACTIVITIES

Activity 1—Adopt A Fishing Area

Take an active part in eliminating trash from your favorite water resource. Adopt a part of or all of a local pond or stream. Adopting means that you assume responsibility for this area all of the time. During your fishing time or during periodic checks, pick up all trash that you can safely reach. Monitor the water quality and watch for changes that might be brought on by runoff from agricultural activities, leakage of waste from local industries, or the dumping of improperly treated human sewage into a body of water. If you suspect a problem, check with the local Department of Health, the Environmental Protection Agency (EPA), or the State Department of Natural Resources.

Activity 2—Take It To The Legislature

Watch your local newspaper for issues that might change the quality of your local aquatic environments. If you see problems, contact local officials or state representatives. Some local conservation organizations publish upcoming legislative initiatives. You might want to get your name on their mailing lists. If you are concerned about an issue, either call or write your congressmen. Most appreciate your sharing your views with them.

Activity 3—Prevention of Overharvest

To prevent the overharvesting of fish, fishing regulations must be followed. Find out from your bait shop or Department of Natural Resources what the regulations are and abide by them. Therefore, if you see individuals who aren't adhering to the regulations, you are obligated to contact your local conservation agencies. Even if the regulations allow for taking a certain number of fish, it is important to use your own judgment for the particular body of water you are fishing and decide whether you should catch and release or if it's okay to catch and eat.

CHAPTER 10

FISH BIOLOGY

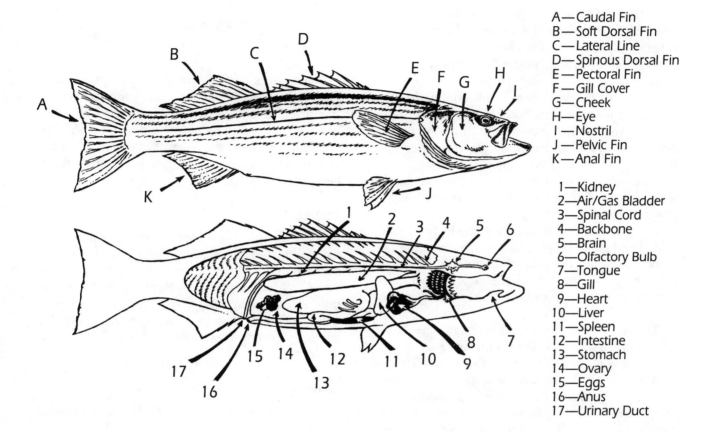

A—Caudal Fin
B—Soft Dorsal Fin
C—Lateral Line
D—Spinous Dorsal Fin
E—Pectoral Fin
F—Gill Cover
G—Cheek
H—Eye
I —Nostril
J —Pelvic Fin
K—Anal Fin

1—Kidney
2—Air/Gas Bladder
3—Spinal Cord
4—Backbone
5—Brain
6—Olfactory Bulb
7—Tongue
8—Gill
9—Heart
10—Liver
11—Spleen
12—Intestine
13—Stomach
14—Ovary
15—Eggs
16—Anus
17—Urinary Duct

WHAT IS A FISH?

All fish are aquatic. This means that although some fish can spend time out of water, all fish must return to water to breathe and to keep from drying out; however, not all creatures that live in water are fish. So, what is a fish?

- **Fish are cold-blooded animals**. Cold-blooded means they have a body temperature that is close to that of the water in which they live.
- Fish are the only **vertebrates** (animals with a backbone) that are able to live in water without breathing air from the atmosphere.

- Their bodies are supported by a **skeleton**, made up of bone or cartilage, and a brain case (cranium) holds the brain.
- Fish have **permanent gills** to extract dissolved oxygen from water. Most fish also have fins, scales, a slimy mucous coating, and a swim bladder.

Fish have been on earth for more than 400 million years. Today there are about 21,000 species! Fish live in water from a few inches deep to as far as five miles beneath the ocean's surface. Fish live in waters from the North and South Poles to the Equator.

Fish come in many sizes, shapes, and colors. Different species prefer different aquatic environments (surroundings) and live their lives in different ways. The more you know about fish, the better angler you'll become.

ANATOMY OF FISH

Fins

Fins make it possible for a fish to stay upright, move, and maneuver in water. Fins are thin membranes usually supported by rays or hard, sharp bony spines.

The **dorsal** fin, which extends vertically from the back, and the **anal** fin, which is just behind the anus at the rear of the belly, help fish keep their balance and move in tight places. Some dorsal fins are spiny-rayed, meaning that they have hard, bony projections separated by membrane. Others are soft-rayed, in which the supports are supple and not hard. Fish may have one, two, or three dorsal fins that can be a combination of spiny and soft rays that may or may not be connected.

The **pectoral** fins found on each side of a fish's body just behind its gills help a fish remain in one place and to dive or swim to the surface. The pectoral fins act like the bow planes on a submarine on fast-swimming fish, helping the fish dive or surface quickly.

The **pelvic** fins are found on each side of the belly and aid in positioning and balance.

The **caudal**, or tail fin helps fish move. This fin also reveals much about a fish's speed and maneuverability. Species of fish with a forked tail are fast swimmers. Fish having broad, flat tails, such as largemouth bass, are able to turn and start swimming quickly.

Fish such as salmon, trout, and catfish, have a small fleshy **adipose** fin on their backs behind the dorsal fin.

Scales

The bodies of most fish are covered with scales. Scales help protect a fish's body from disease and injury. Fish don't grow more scales as they get older; the scales just get bigger. As a fish grows, rings appear on the scales. By counting the rings on a single scale, scientists can determine a fish's age, just like counting the rings on the cross-section of a tree trunk.

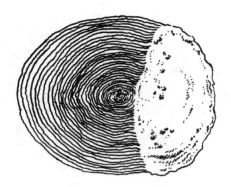

Rings of a Fish Scale

Scales are modified skin cells that have various shapes. Those on sharks are actually tiny teeth called "denticles" and are extremely rough and abrasive. The tarpon has large scales, often larger than a silver dollar. Some of the fastest swimming fish, such as the tuna, salmon, trout, mackerel, and others, have tiny scales.

Mucus

Fish are coated by a mucus (slime) that helps protect them from disease, fungi, and parasites and reduces friction with the water, making it easier to swim. When you plan to release a fish, it's important not to damage this slimy coating. Touching a fish's body can destroy or remove this protective coating. *If you must handle a fish's body, wet your hands first.*

Gills

Why do fish have gills? Fish get the oxygen needed to live from water. The water enters a fish's mouth, which then closes. The operculum, or gill cover, opens slightly and water passes through the gills. In moving water or when a fish swims, the flow of water occurs without aid. When there is no water flow or when the fish is stationary, the flow of water is created by the opening and closing of the

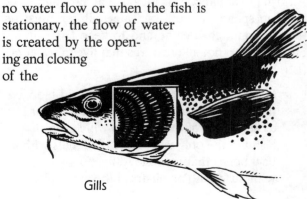

Gills

fish's mouth. As the water passes through the gills, the dissolved oxygen present in the water is removed, and carbon dioxide from the fish's blood is released.

Bony fish have four pairs of gills, while sharks may have as many as seven. *Injury to the gills is often fatal.*

Swim Bladder

Many fish have a swim, or gas bladder, in their bodies. This makes it possible for them to suspend themselves in water and not sink to the bottom. The bladder is an air-tight sac in most fish; in others, fish can add or release gas to remain in deep or shallow water.

Some fish, such as mackerel, shark and tuna, don't have a swim bladder and maintain their position by staying in constant motion.

Skeleton

Most fish have a bony skeleton with various body parts held together and to the skeleton by connective tissue. The skeleton protects a fish's organs and supports the muscles. Because fish are vertebrates, there is a backbone running the length of the body. The location and flexibility of the backbone allows a fish to swim. However, some fish, including lamprey, sturgeons and sharks, have skeletons of cartilage, rather than bone.

Fish with
Bony Skeleton

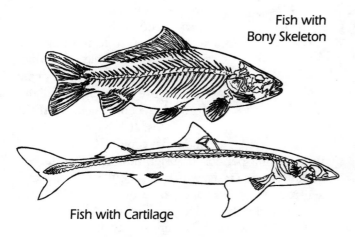

Fish with Cartilage

FISH COLOR

Fish, especially saltwater fish, come in a variety of body colors and patterns. Almost every species is counter-shaded, dark across the back and light on the belly. This protective coloring helps them stay hidden from both their predators and their prey.

In most cases, the coloration of fish allows them to blend in with the place they live. For example, the upper part of the bullhead, which spends much of its time near bottom, is dark. So, from above it's difficult to see a bullhead against the muddy bottom of a river or a lake. The color pattern of northern pike resembles sunlight filtering through a weed bed. This enables them to hide there to ambush their food. The adaptive coloration also helps conceal the fish from birds and other predators.

HOW FISH SWIM

Most fish swim by moving their bodies in a series of wavy, snake-like motions. Each motion ends with a snap of the tail.

Some fish can swim extremely fast. Members of the tuna family can swim up to 50 miles an hour by snapping their powerful forked tails as much as 20 times a second! Each tail snap moves a tuna about the length of its body. There are variations  among species, but one can estimate that the top speed of a fish is about seven miles per hour per foot of body length.

THE SENSES OF FISH

Understanding how a fish hears, sees, and smells will help you catch more fish.

The senses of some species are better developed than those of others. Some fish use their sense of smell to find food. Eels and salmon are well known for their ability to smell. Other fish, such as bonefish, sturgeon, and catfish, use their sense of taste to feed. Catfish have taste buds on their "whiskers" or barbels and can taste food even before taking it into their mouths. Many fish use their senses of sight and hearing to feed. These include barracuda, billfish, striped bass, and trout. Sharks use the senses of sight, sound, and smell to feed.

How Fish Hear

What Fish Hear. Sound travels through water at a rate of about one mile per second. This is five times faster than its speed through air. Fish have superb hearing, especially low-frequency sounds. This is why anglers talk about the need to move quietly on the bank of a pond or in a boat. A moving school of baitfish sends out sound waves that travel quickly through the water. The noise of a tackle box scraped along the deck of a boat is echoed through the water. Footsteps along a bank send vibrations into the water. Some fish can even hear the sound made by a live worm wriggling on the bottom. Fish have become adept at detecting and reacting to these sounds that signal food or danger.

Ears. Fish have ears located beneath the skin on either side of the head. Sound reaches a fish's ears through its skin, flesh, and bone. In some species, there is an internal connection between the ear and the swim bladder that acts as a resonator and amplifier, which is particularly helpful in detecting very low or soft sounds. The ears of a fish receive far-field sound.

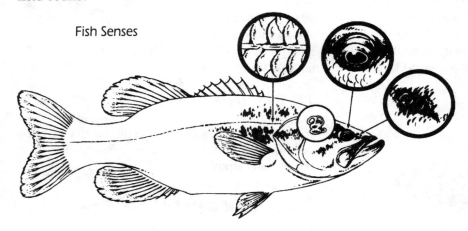

Fish Senses

Acoustico-lateral System. Fish also have a second sound-detecting system called the lateral line which deals with near-field low frequency sounds caused by the displacement of water. No other vertebrate has this organ, which responds to strong, low-frequency vibrations in water within a 20- to 30-foot range. Sometimes it is called the **sense of distant touch** because it is incredibly directional and accurate. With it, a fish can locate and strike a black lure on a moonless night in turbid water!

The lateral line begins just behind the head and extends almost to the tail along each side of a fish's body. On most species, it can be seen. The lateral line consists of a series of canals lined with sound sensors called "neuromasts," which are sensitive to low-frequency sounds. The neuromasts have pods of tiny, sensory hairs connected to nerve fiber that leads to the fish's brain.

Near-field sound occurs when molecules of water are disturbed and pushed. Imagine the small waves of water caused when a rock is thrown into the water and how the waves get smaller further away from the splash. As fish or other animals swim through the water, they push the water, creating a disturbance similar to the rock. This slight movement of water disturbs the neuromasts, which send signals to the brain. Far-field sound, "heard" by a fish's ears, takes place when water molecules are moved but are too distant to be pushed far enough in one direction to disturb the neuromasts.

How Fish See

Fish first use their sense of hearing or smell to find food, but they usually use their sight to make a final attack. The eyes of fish are fixed and cannot open or close because they have no eyelids! The eyes are also round and located on the sides of the head. This makes fish **nearsighted**. Objects at short distances can be seen clearly, but objects farther away are blurry. Fish, however, can see nearly all around them except for a small area directly behind them.

Because fish do not have an iris, they often avoid areas that are too bright or dark. They can also adjust to changes in light through receptor cells in their eyes. Most fish have both cone and rod receptors. Cone cells are used during periods of brightness. During darker conditions, the rods, which are about 30 times more sensitive than the cones, take over. However, the rods record only in black and white.

Can fish see colors? Scientists say they can. Many species of fish can see at least 24 different shades of colors.

How Fish Smell

The sense of smell is important for many fish. They use smell to find food, sense danger, and find their way to distant spawning areas.

All fish have at least two nostrils, called **nares**, in their snouts. Most gamefish have four nares, two on each side of the snout. Behind the nares is a chamber lined with sensors that can detect the slightest odor.

Fish that live on the bottom or in very deep water rely heavily on their sense of smell. But it is also important to fish that inhabit shallow water. Species with a well-developed sense of smell have an advantage feeding at night. Catfish, for instance, have a good sense of smell and often provide anglers with great fishing after dark.

Smell is also used to detect the presence of enemies. Coho and chinook salmon can detect incredibly small amounts of odor from seals and sea lions. During one test, these fish detected this odor in concentrations so low that it would be like detecting two-hundredths of a single drop in a 23,000 gallon swimming pool. It is also the salmon's sense of smell that allows this species to travel hundreds of miles to return to the stream of its birth.

Pheromone is the term that describes a smell that is used for a form of communication among fish. Baitfish, for example, often panic at the smell of a wounded member in a school. There is a substance in the skin of baitfish called **schreckstoff**, or **fright substance**, which is visible under a microscope. When a predator grabs or eats a baitfish, this substance is emitted and warns other baitfish to stay clear of the area.

Fish Taste and Touch

Fish have the ability to distinguish between sweet, sour, salty, and bitter. Taste is important to species such as sturgeon and catfish, which can also locate food by touch using barbels, the whiskers around the mouth.

Taste buds of fish are usually external, but there are internal taste buds in some species. Catfish have taste buds all over their body, including the tail, which help them find and select food in muddy or silty water.

Carp also have the ability to taste food externally, as do some saltwater species such as cod and black drum.

Why Understanding Fish Senses Is Important

Most fish are alert to what is happening around them. Once you know how fish feed and how they use their senses, you will become a better angler.

Learning why fish act the way they do is both interesting and important. Once you understand their behavior, you will appreciate fish and their role in nature. You will also become a more successful angler if you learn where fish are most likely to be located at different times of the year, how different species rely on their senses to find food, and what kinds of food each species prefers. You can then use this information to know where and when to fish and what lures or baits to use.

ACTIVITIES

Activity 1—Adaptations for Survival

Cleaning your catch provides a good time to observe characteristics that increase the fish's chances of surviving in an aquatic environment. You are probably already aware that some fish have spines in the dorsal fin that can cause pain if you are stuck with one. Stretch out a fin. Notice the membrane between the spines which provides surface area to push against the water.

See how the large eyes of fish are located on the side of the head and provide a wide range of visibility. Fish lack eyelids, but have a nictitating membrane which protects the eyes from irritants in the water.

Open the mouth and move the corners which are hinged and folded. This arrangement allows the mouth to open wide to accommodate large bait fish. Stick a straight object as far as it will go into the mouth of the fish. Look into the mouth and note that the mouth, esophagus and stomach are lined up in such a manner that the front of the fish's dinner can be in the stomach with the back end hanging out of its mouth.

IDENTIFICATION OF COMMON SPORT FISH

How Many Species of Fish Can You Identify in this Montage? (See bottom of page 79 for the species of fish included in the Montage.)

WHAT KIND OF FISH IS THIS?

Everyone should know the names of the fish they catch. Studying pictures of fish can help you learn, but seeing live fish is better. Once you have seen a live fish a few times, you will recognize the family to which it belongs. Later, you can try to identify the exact species. For example, after catching a few bass, it will be easy to identify a bass. Later you will be able to tell whether the fish is a largemouth or a smallmouth bass.

Fish have two kinds of names. One is a common name. It isn't unusual for the same fish to have

many common names, depending on the state where it is found, but a fish has only one scientific name. For example, common names for the largemouth bass include bigmouth bass, black bass, largemouth black bass, green bass, and bayou bass. Its scientific name, however, is always **Micropterus salmoides**.

Most anglers learn to identify fish by sight. Some fish are easy to identify. Others may be more difficult because some species look alike. To tell the difference between similar species, anglers look closely at the shape, pattern, color, fins, mouth, and other characteristics that help tell what kind of fish it is.

SOME COMMON FRESHWATER FISH

The Sunfish Family (Centrarchidae)

North America has 30 species of fish that are members of the sunfish family. The key to identifying sunfish is the dorsal fin on their back. All members of this family have a dorsal fin with two connected parts. The front portion has stiff spines while the rear portion has soft rays.

The sunfish family can be separated into three groups—sunfishes, crappies, and the black basses.

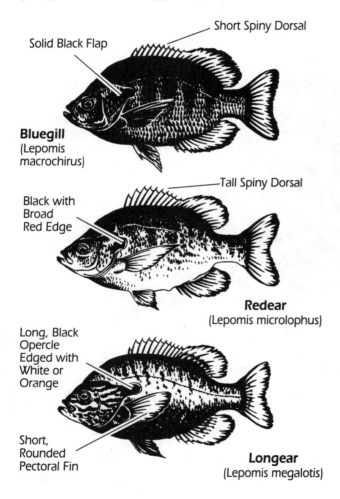

Short Spiny Dorsal

Solid Black Flap

Bluegill
(Lepomis macrochirus)

Tall Spiny Dorsal

Black with Broad Red Edge

Redear
(Lepomis microlophus)

Long, Black Opercle Edged with White or Orange

Short, Rounded Pectoral Fin

Longear
(Lepomis megalotis)

Sunfishes. The sunfishes include such fish as the bluegill, redear, and longear. The bluegill can be identified by the solid black flap on the gill cover and a dark blotch at the back of the dorsal fin. The redear can be identified by the flap on the gill cover which is black with a broad red stripe. The longear has a long black flap on the gill cover with a white margin. The number of common names for bluegill will amaze you. In some areas the bluegill and other sunfish are called bream, roach, sunnies, kivvers, and johnny-roach!

Crappies. The crappies are the white crappie and the black crappie. Black and white crappies look much alike. Usually, the black crappie has many dark blotches on its body while the white crappie is more silvery with black markings that form seven to nine vertical bars on the sides of its body. To make sure, you can count the spines in the dorsal fin. Black crappies have seven or eight. White crappies have only six.

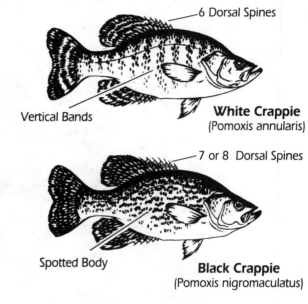

6 Dorsal Spines

Vertical Bands

White Crappie
(Pomoxis annularis)

7 or 8 Dorsal Spines

Spotted Body

Black Crappie
(Pomoxis nigromaculatus)

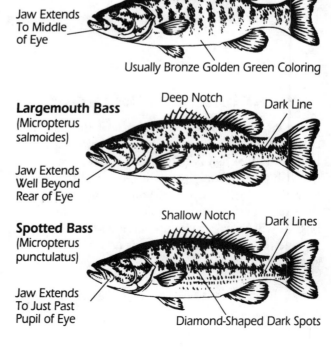

Smallmouth Bass
(Micropterus dolomieui)

Shallow Notch

Jaw Extends To Middle of Eye

Usually Bronze Golden Green Coloring

Largemouth Bass
(Micropterus salmoides)

Deep Notch

Dark Line

Jaw Extends Well Beyond Rear of Eye

Spotted Bass
(Micropterus punctulatus)

Shallow Notch

Dark Lines

Jaw Extends To Just Past Pupil of Eye

Diamond-Shaped Dark Spots

Black Basses. The black basses include the largemouth, smallmouth, redeye, and spotted bass. To tell the difference between largemouth bass and smallmouth bass, study the jaw. On the largemouth, the jaw extends back beyond the eye. The jaw of the smallmouth, however, extends just behind the pupil of the eye. Another way to tell the difference is to look at the dorsal fin. Smallmouth bass have a shallow notch between the spiny and soft-rayed sections. Largemouth have a sharp notch at this same place.

Trout and Salmon (Salmonidae)

Trout and salmon belong to a family of fish known as Salmonidae. There are 39 different North American species in the Salmonidae family and all have a fleshy adipose fin between the dorsal fin and the tail.

Scientists break down the family Salmonidae into several groups. The major groups of interest to the angler include trouts, chars, Pacific salmon, grayling, and whitefish.

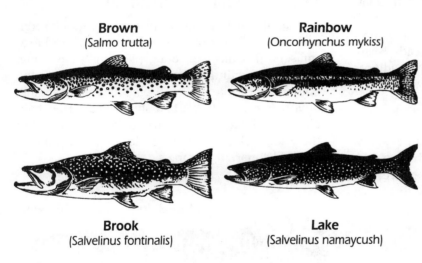

Brown
(Salmo trutta)

Rainbow
(Oncorhynchus mykiss)

Brook
(Salvelinus fontinalis)

Lake
(Salvelinus namaycush)

Trouts. The true trouts include the brown trout, golden trout, cutthroat trout, Apache trout, Gila trout, and Atlantic Salmon. Generally true trouts have darker spots on a lighter background, while chars have lighter spots on a darker background. Cutthroat trout, common in the western states, are identified by a red slash mark under the lower jaw.

Chars. The chars include brook trout, lake trout, Dolly Varden, and bull trout. The brook trout has worm-like markings on its back and pink or reddish fins edged with white. Dolly Vardens have red, orange or yellow spots. Lake trout have very pale spots on the body and on the dorsal fin, anal fin, and the tail.

Pacific Salmon

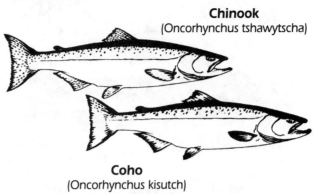

Chinook
(Oncorhynchus tshawytscha)

Coho
(Oncorhynchus kisutch)

Pacific Salmon. Pacific salmon include the chinook, chum, sockeye, pink, coho, and the steelhead/rainbow trout. The chinook is also called the king salmon and the coho is also called the silver salmon. These fish are found from California to Alaska. In addition, they have been stocked in the Great Lakes and in some other large, freshwater lakes and reservoirs. The rainbow trout is also stocked in coldwater lakes, rivers and streams throughout North America.

Pacific salmon are **anadromous** fish. This means they live in saltwater, but move into freshwater streams and rivers to spawn. Depending on the time spent in a river, their body color changes from bright silver to dark or brilliant hues. Most rainbow trout are not anadromous. Rainbow that do migrate to the ocean are known as steelhead.

Whitefish and Grayling. Within the lower 48 states, the whitefishes and grayling live in a limited area in the northern and western states. They are widely distributed in Alaska and Canada.

The Catfish Family (Ictalurdae)

Catfish have smooth skin with no scales. Catfish, however, have "whiskers" or barbels around their mouths that contain many taste buds. Catfish can actually taste their food before they put it into their mouth. Catfish have sharp spines on the dorsal and pectoral fins. If one of these spines punctures your skin, it can cause a painful wound.

75

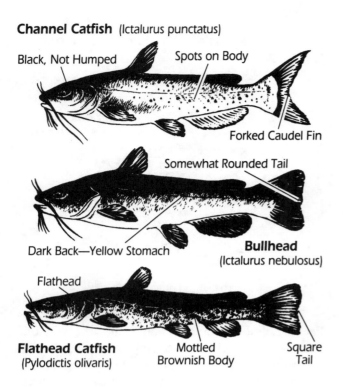

Channel Catfish (Ictalurus punctatus)

Black, Not Humped

Spots on Body

Forked Caudel Fin

Somewhat Rounded Tail

Dark Back—Yellow Stomach

Bullhead
(Ictalurus nebulosus)

Flathead

Flathead Catfish
(Pylodictis olivaris)

Mottled
Brownish Body

Square
Tail

Yellow Perch
(Perca flavescens)

Vertical Bars

Walleye
(Stizostedion
vitreum)

No Spots

Large, Glassy Eye

White Tip

Sauger
(Stizostedion
canadense)

Spots on
Dorsal Fin

Large, Glassy Eye

Bullheads, which are members of the catfish family, have rounded tails, while channel and blue catfish have forked tails. The flathead catfish has an almost square tail, similar in appearance to bullheads. Members of the catfish family also have a large adipose fin between the dorsal fin and the tail.

The Perch Family (Percidae)

The members of the perch family include yellow perch, walleye, and sauger. Yellow perch have dark backs, yellowish to golden sides, and dark vertical bands on the back and sides. The dorsal fin is split into two parts, and their lower fins may be reddish or orange.

Walleye and sauger are difficult to tell apart. Their bodies are round and they have slightly forked tails. You can tell them apart by looking at the spiny dorsal fin. The walleye has a large dark blotch near the base of the last few spines and dark streaks throughout the dorsal fin. The sauger has distinct dark spots throughout the dorsal fin, but no blotch.

They both have sharp teeth and large, glassy eyes. These features allow them to feed on fish. Their bodies are olive-green to golden on the sides and their bellies are white. The tail of a walleye has a silver or white tip. The sauger doesn't have this feature.

The Pike Family (Esocidae)

This family includes chain pickerel, grass pickerel, red fin pickerel, northern pike, and muskellunge (muskie). The members of the pike family have long, slim bodies with the dorsal fin set well back on the body near a forked tail. All pike have long snouts, *almost like a duck bill*, and sharp teeth. The chain pickerel, which grows to nine pounds, is larger than the grass pickerel or red fin pickerel. It has black, chain-like marking on the sides.

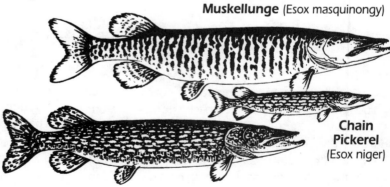

Muskellunge (Esox masquinongy)

**Chain
Pickerel**
(Esox niger)

Northern Pike (Esox lucius)

The northern pike has bean-shaped spots on its side and dark spots on fins and the tail, while the muskellunge has vertical bars on its body. The entire head of a muskie has scales. On the northern pike, only the upper half of the gill cover has scales. If you look under the jaws of both fish, there are tiny holes. The pike has five on each side. The muskie has six to nine on each side. Pike grow to 50 pounds while muskie may reach 60 pounds!

SOME COMMON SALTWATER FISH

Billfish (Istiophoridae)

This is the name given to a group of large fish that live in temperate and tropical waters. They all have long, pointed upper jaws that form a "spear" or a "sword." Billfish include the **marlins, sailfish, swordfish,** and **spearfish.** Billfish are easy to identify if you study their fins. The sailfish has a large dorsal

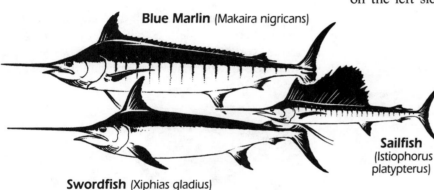

Blue Marlin (Makaira nigricans)

Sailfish (Istiophorus platypterus)

Swordfish (Xiphias gladius)

fin on its back that is taller than the deepest part of its body.

Blue, striped, and black marlin have pointed dorsal fins, but there are other differences. The black marlin has rigid pectoral fins. They don't fold back like the ones on the blue and striped marlins. The pointed front of the dorsal fin on the striped marlin is higher than that on the blue. Also, the blue marlin has a much higher anal fin than the striped marlin. White marlin have a rounded dorsal fin. The swordfish has a very long, wide bill and a high, curved dorsal fin.

Flounder (order Pleuronectiformes)

Flounder belong to a group of flatfishes that live on the sandy or muddy bottoms of bays and along the shores of most oceans. They have a dark, mottled coloring on one side of their body that helps them hide from predators. The other side is white. These

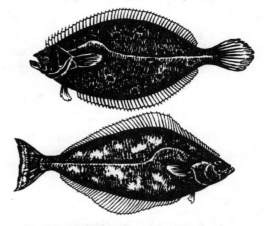

Summer Flounder (Paralichthys dentatus)

Pacific Halibut (Hippoglossus stenolepis)

fish swim on their right side. Some have both eyes on the left side of their bodies. Others have both eyes on the right side. This characteristic helps identify particular species.

Cods (Gadidae)

Members of the cod family are found in cold northern and Arctic waters. Most live in shallow waters near coasts, but can be caught in deep water. Almost all cods live on the bottom. They have small scales and soft-rayed fins. Usually they have a large mouth and a barbel on the chin.

Cod family members include the Atlantic cod, tomcod, hake, pollack, and haddock. The only freshwater cod is the burbot. They inhabit cold, deep northern lakes.

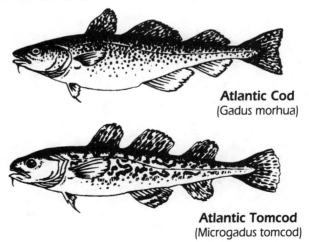

Atlantic Cod (Gadus morhua)

Atlantic Tomcod (Microgadus tomcod)

Dolphin (Coryphaeeena hippurus)

Dolphin, also known by its Hawaiian name mahi-mahi, are found in tropical and sub-tropical waters. Along the Atlantic Coast of the U.S., it is found in areas influenced by the warm waters of the Gulf Stream. After a dolphin is caught, its colors fluctuate, but in the water it is usually a vivid greenish-blue with dark vertical bands that appear and disappear. Certain porpoises are also known as "dolphin," but these are mammals, not fishes.

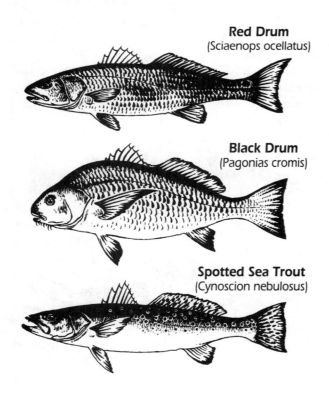

Dolphin
(Coryphaeeena hippurus)

The Drum Family (Sciaenidae)

Drums are found throughout the world, generally in temperate and tropical waters. Usually, they live over sandy bottoms in shallow water near estuaries. They have a lateral line on the sides of the body that extends onto the tail fin. Usually, drums have one or more barbels on the lower jaw.

Red Drum
(Sciaenops ocellatus)

Black Drum
(Pagonias cromis)

Spotted Sea Trout
(Cynoscion nebulosus)

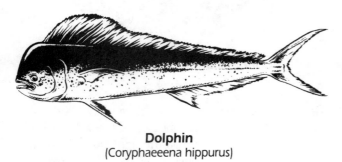

Members of the drum family include the red drum, black drum, spotted seatrout, common weakfish, corvina, spot, and croakers.

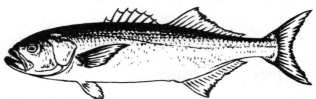

Bluefish (Pomatomous saltatrix)

Bluefish (Pomatomous saltatrix)

Bluefish range in size from 1 to over 20 pounds. They are a bright silver and blue color and have powerful jaws lined with sharp teeth. Bluefish eat eels and small fish that they encounter in their travels.

More anglers pursue bluefish than any other fish on the east coast of the U.S., although their distribution is worldwide. Atlantic Coast fish winter in warm waters off Florida and migrate all the way to Maine by summer's end.

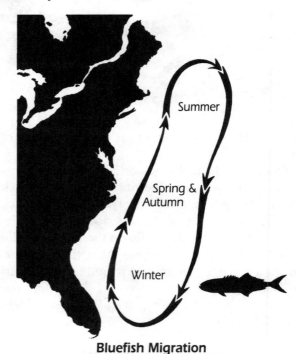

Summer

Spring & Autumn

Winter

Bluefish Migration

The adults spawn in warmer southern waters. The juveniles, called snapper blues, head north in the sprin just before the adults. West coast bluefish make similar seasonal migrations along the Pacific Coast.

Rockfish (Scorpaenidae)

A variety of species caught along West Coast shores are known collectively as "rockfish." Popular favorites are black rockfish, quillback rockfish, copper rockfish, and yelloweye rockfish. Other fish caught in the same areas are greenlings, lingcod, sculpins, and dogfish (a shark).

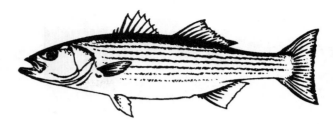

Striped Bass (Morone saxatilis)

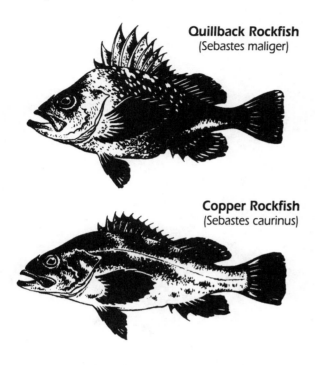

Quillback Rockfish
(Sebastes maliger)

Copper Rockfish
(Sebastes caurinus)

ANADROMOUS FISH

Anadromous fish are fish that live in saltwater and in the Great Lakes, but move into freshwater streams and rivers to spawn. Anadromous fish include fish in a variety of families. They include striped bass, shad, Atlantic and Pacific salmon, and some sturgeon. Some species of trout and char, including the rainbow or steelhead trout, brown trout, Dolly Varden, brook trout, and cutthroat trout move from freshwater streams and rivers to the ocean or large freshwater lakes for a period of time where they grow at a much faster rate. These are called "sea-run" or "lake-run" fish.

ACTIVITIES

Activity 1—Knowing Your Fish

To become acquainted with the types of sport fish found in your area, visit a local bait shop or the visitor center in a nearby state park. Various species of sport fish are often mounted or displayed.

Another good place to visit is the fish cleaning area of your local marina. Also, many zoos have special displays that include the habitat and fish species found in that area.

As you view each species, write down the names of the fish and note any characteristics which can be used to distinguish between species. Characteristics which you might use are the shape and location of fins, coloration, and fish shape.

Activity 2—Resources for Fish Identification

There are a number of places that provide resources to aid in fish identification. Federal agencies and State Departments of Natural Resources often have pamphlets or booklets which aid in identification. Some state universities maintain extension agencies which have a supply of such material. Don't forget your public library for books devoted to fish. Even some sets of encyclopedias have colored pictures which identify different species.

The species of fish in the montage on page 73 are: head = Bull Dolphin; whiskers = Catfish or Bullhead; gill cover = Bluegill; anal/ventral fin = Largemouth Bass; spots = Spotted Sea Trout; dorsal fin = Sailfish; tail = Sturgeon; pectoral fin = Blue Marlin

CHAPTER 12

FOOD CHAINS AND ECOLOGY

Food Chain

If you like to fish for largemouth bass, you may think that all you need to do is learn about largemouth bass. But to know largemouth bass, you have to know the following things about a largemouth's habitat:

- How is a largemouth bass affected by non-living things such as water, temperature, pH, and chemicals?
- How is a largemouth bass affected by other living things in the water such as plants, other fish, and other animals?
- How is a largemouth bass affected by living things around the pond such as birds and humans?

- How is a largemouth bass affected by non-living things that come into water such as soil, pesticides, and trash?

This is what **ecology** is all about. **Ecology is the study of the relationships of organisms with other organisms and non-living factors.**

The world is made up of ecosystems, which are complex networks, or webs, of interrelated and interdependent animals, plants, and the habitat in which they live. In this chapter you will learn how both non-living and living organisms relate to the fish.

RELATIONSHIP TO LIVING ORGANISMS—AQUATIC FOOD CHAINS AND WEBS

All living organisms belong to "food chains." A food chain is made up of a series of organisms that produce and consume food. It is the path that food (materials and energy) takes through a group of organisms.

For example, a food chain may begin with tiny floating plants (**phytoplankton**) and small animals (**zooplankton**) that eat the plants. The next step in the chain may be small fish like bluegill that eat the small organisms and then largemouth bass that eat bluegills. The final step may be an angler who catches and eats the largemouth bass, or a crayfish that eats the largemouth bass after it has died.

An **ecosystem** is more complex than this example. An ecosystem may have hundreds of food chains intertwined and linked together. Largemouth bass, for instance, do not feed only on bluegill so they are part of other food chains. Other big fish like northern pike eat bluegill, so bluegill are part of other food chains. Everything is a part of a "food web."

Food chains link together to form **food webs**. If you affect any one part of that web, you affect everything in the web. If you take away or pollute the water, the bluegill cannot survive. But what if you take away the plants? The bluegill does not feed on plants, but it feeds on the insects and other organisms that eat the plants. If the plants are gone, then the insects are also gone. Also, if you take away the plants, where will the bluegill hide from bigger fish? What will happen to the bigger fish if the bluegill are gone?

To further understand this, it helps to know the different roles played in the food chain. In a lake or an ocean, living organisms are either **producers** or **consumers of food.**

Producers

Green plants and algae are producers. They use water and the energy from the sun to produce their own food through a process called **photosynthesis**. Plants produce oxygen when bathed in sunlight.

Plants have the ability to manufacture sugars, fats, proteins, and other compounds from basic inorganic materials and sunlight. Animals don't have the abil-

ity to do this. Some of this food is used by plants for their own survival. The amount of excess food is the amount available for other life forms.

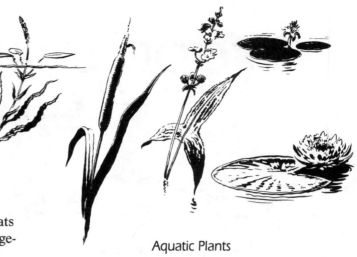

Aquatic Plants

Plants are the basis of all life on earth! They form the broad base of the food chain. Animals could not live without green plants. Rooted plants are extremely visible, but the food chain usually begins with one-celled microscopic organisms. They are almost impossible to see with the naked eye. These plants are called **phytoplankton. Plankton** is a general term for all of the small life forms in the water.

A significant amount of the food produced at the base of the food chain is not utilized because not all of the plants and the phytoplankton are eaten. Some die of natural causes, but this is important, too, because, in the process, vital nutrients are returned to the ecosystem.

If animals throughout the food chain are to survive, there must always be more food than necessary at each level. This allows the food sources to reproduce and renew themselves. If they were completely destroyed or seriously diminished in a given area, it would have a catastrophic effect on higher organisms that depend on the food chain for their survival.

Consumers

Animals and non-green plants cannot make their own food and cannot be considered self-sufficient. They are called **heterotrophs**, meaning that they are other-nourished.

Animals are consumers. Some animals, called primary-consumers or herbivores, feed on plant life.

Some **herbivores** are extremely small animals called **zooplankton** that feed on microscopic plants. Other examples of herbivores are insects, worms, shrimp, and some fish.

The food taken from plants by herbivores, or first-order consumers, must not only provide energy, but also very specific organic compounds and nutrients. The absence of any of these for a brief period will stop the production of protein. A long-term lack can result in death.

Carnivores are meat eaters and form the second order of consumers. Scientists call the carnivores that consume small plant and animal organisms **foragers**. Many pan fish such as bluegill and crappie fall into this category along with crayfish, shiners, crabs, alewives, and menhaden.

The next-higher level carnivores are **predators**. Most of the game fish that many anglers want to catch including pike, muskie, bass, trout, salmon, tuna, tarpon, and bluefish are predators. Each species of fish relates in a number of ways to other species of fish. Each species relates to others it hunts for food, to others it competes with for food, and to those for which it is food. At some time in its life, every fish can be considered a predator—a fish that preys on another animal. Bluegill, often the prey of largemouth bass, raid the nests of the bass and eat the eggs. Also, after bass eggs hatch, bluegill will eat newly hatched bass fry. Through this reversal of the predator-prey relationship, fish populations are kept in check.

Predator fish try to stay close to their prey. Some lie in ambush until a victim comes close. The prey is

Fishing for Tautog (Blackfish) Using Crabs in Rocky Habitat

captured as the predator bursts from its hiding place. Barracuda, flounder, largemouth bass, muskie, northern pike, and trout often do this. Other predators search under rocks for food. Tautog (blackfish) searching for crabs or smallmouth bass chasing crayfish are good examples. Still other predator fish swim, sometimes in schools, to find prey. Many kinds of saltwater fish such as tuna, bluefish, and mackerel do this.

Some fish's diets change as they grow older. Very young bass may eat algae and microscopic animals at first, but switch to insects, smaller fish and other animals as they grow older.

It is within this second order of consumers that the delicate balance in nature becomes more obvious. If carnivores consume most of their food supply, they and their offspring will starve. That would allow the first order consumers to reestablish so that the balance can be achieved once again. Seldom, however, does a carnivore totally eliminate its food supply because few depend on a single food source for survival.

Finally, human beings are the highest-order consumers, eating organisms from all the levels below them.

Decomposers

Decomposers are things like bacteria and other microbes that break down dead plants and animals. As dead plants and animals decay through this process, they release basic nutrients back into the system. These nutrients are used by plants during photosynthesis and also by animals.

Decomposers can stay dormant for long periods, conserving their energy and waiting for the opportunity to feed on dead plants or animals. But once

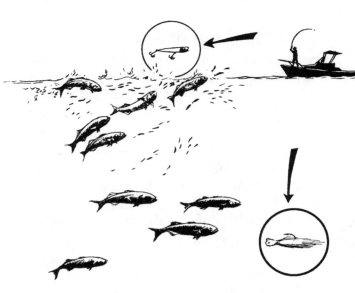

Fishing for Bluefish

food is present, they multiply at an incredible rate. Even the wastes from the decomposers are used and broken down further by other organisms.

Energy Flow

Energy flow is the medium of exchange for any ecosystem. Within any food chain, there is a transfer of energy. Radiant energy from the sun is vital to green plants. This energy is stored by green plants as sugars or carbohydrates.

The chemical energy used at each level of the food chain is not recoverable. At each level, there is less energy available than at the level below. This is an important concept and involves the 10 percent rule—only 10 percent of the useful energy at one level will be passed on to the next higher level. This creates a pyramid with a broad base, steep sides, and a peak. Top predators, especially those that are exciting to catch, are at the pyramid's peak. This is why there are so few of them as compared to baitfish and other creatures at lower levels of the pyramid.

For example, walleye require a large area in which to forage and there are seldom many of them in any lake or river. To produce and sustain a single 10-pound walleye requires about 100 pounds of perch annually. One hundred pounds of perch depends on one-half ton of minnows. Those minnows rely on five tons of worms and insects for their survival. The worms and insects need 50 tons of plants for their support. In this example of the pyramid mentioned earlier, it takes 50 tons of plants for one 10-pound walleye. Now you can see how valuable one large gamefish is!

Although much of the energy flow within an ecosystem is lost, certain chemicals and nutrients must be recycled if the process of generating new energy is to continue.

Population Dynamics

Under normal conditions, the populations of a given fish species contains members of various sizes. Most fish lay large numbers of eggs, but only a relatively few become adults. Many eggs, fry, and fingerlings don't survive to maturity.

Sunfish form random schools, while true schooling species such as trout, salmon, and shad remain in schools of their year-class, or hatching year. All members are similar in size. As the fish age, schools become smaller because of predation, disease and other causes. The population dynamics of a given species is shaped like the pyramid of the food chain. The smaller fish of the species are more numerous.

RELATIONSHIP TO NON-LIVING ENVIRONMENTAL CONDITIONS

Fish are found nearly everywhere there is water with enough food, oxygen and cover. However, not all fish can live in the same kind of waters. Different species can tolerate different environmental conditions and have different habitat needs, including:

- Amounts of salt
- Amounts of oxygen
- Types and amounts of food (described above)
- Water temperature
- Hiding areas (cover and the bottom)
- Breeding areas (See Chapter 13)
- Water Quality

Salinity (Amount of Salt)

One major factor that separates fish is salt. Some fish cannot live in areas where there is a high salt level and others need salt in the water to live. However, some fish can live in both saltwater and freshwater!

Fresh Water. Fresh water contains much less salt than the ocean. Most ponds, reservoirs, and rivers across North America are fresh water. Some common freshwater fish are bluegills, carp, catfish, crappie, bass, perch, northern pike, trout, and walleye.

Salt Water. Many kinds of fish live in the salty water of the oceans. A fish's kidney keeps the proper balance of salt in its body. Popular saltwater fish are bluefish, cod, flounder, striped bass (also found in fresh

Food Pyramid

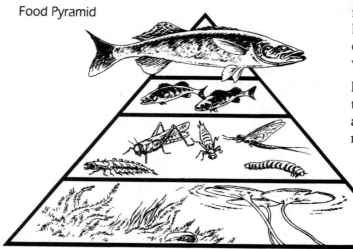

water), sea trout, tarpon, tuna, halibut, rockfish, seaperch, lingcod, and yellowtail.

Brackish Water. An estuary is where freshwater streams and rivers meet the salt water from the ocean. The amount of salt (salinity) changes daily with the flow of tides, rain, or drought. This water is termed *brackish*. Changes in the amount of salinity will determine which fish can live in the area. Species found in these waters include redfish, sea trout, snook, and striped bass.

Some fish live in salt water, but swim up freshwater streams and rivers to spawn (lay their eggs). These fish are called **anadromous fish.** They include shad, salmon, and some kinds of trout.

Oxygen

Without an adequate supply of oxygen in the water, fish cannot survive. Fish such as carp can live on less oxygen than fish like trout. What can affect the amount of oxygen in the water? Living plants within a lake or stream add oxygen to the water through **photosynthesis**—the process of using sunlight to make food. Oxygen can also enter water from the surrounding air. In a stream, moving water tumbling over rocks picks up oxygen from the air.

Decaying plants use oxygen from the water to decompose, thus decreasing oxygen levels. Pollution of many kinds reduces oxygen in water. Chemicals dumped into water trap oxygen and take it out of the natural system. Thermal pollution, the heating of water through industrial use, reduces the amount of oxygen water can hold. Water temperature affects the amount of oxygen that water can hold. Colder water can hold more oxygen molecules than warm water. Oxygen levels change from one location to another in the same body of water.

Water Temperature

Each fish has a different range of water temperature in which it can survive. Some fish can live in a wide range of temperatures, but trout require cold water. Although fish cannot always find the exact temperature they prefer, they are usually found in water close to that temperature.

There also is an important relationship between oxygen and temperature. Fish require more oxygen in warmer water, yet as water gets warmers, it contains less oxygen. Water temperature is perhaps the single, most important factor in determining where fish will be and how they will behave. Each species

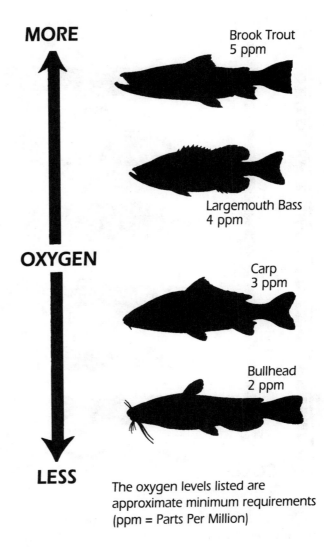

MORE

OXYGEN

LESS

Brook Trout
5 ppm

Largemouth Bass
4 ppm

Carp
3 ppm

Bullhead
2 ppm

The oxygen levels listed are approximate minimum requirements (ppm = Parts Per Million)

also has its own comfort and tolerance level. Fish tend to seek the most comfortable environment, assuming that there is sufficient oxygen.

As temperatures change, shallow water areas warm and cool more quickly than deeper water. Bass anglers know that early in the season, some of the best fishing occurs in coves and backwaters because temperatures are slightly warmer than in deeper water areas. However, during a cold snap, fish leave the shallows for the depths, but will return when warmer weather returns. However, when the water becomes too warm, the fish will tend to migrate to deeper water where temperatures are moderate. This migration from the shallows to the depths occurs not only seasonally, but within a twenty-four hour period during summer months as the fish move to the shallows in the morning and evening, while moving to the depths during the hot daylight hours.

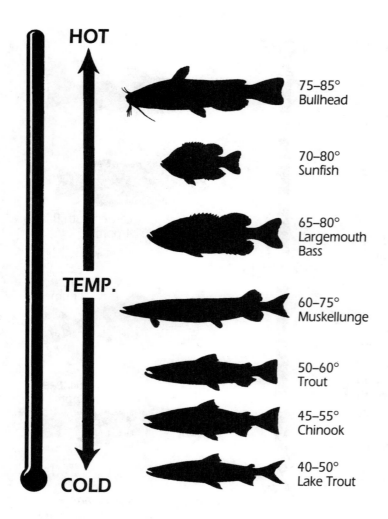

HOT

75–85°
Bullhead

70–80°
Sunfish

65–80°
Largemouth
Bass

TEMP.

60–75°
Muskellunge

50–60°
Trout

45–55°
Chinook

40–50°
Lake Trout

COLD

The temperatures shown are optimum ranges. However, all of these fish may survive in near freezing water temperatures.

Cover

Cover, such as aquatic plants, rocks, logs, or any other type of cover, is a requirement for many fish. Fish seek cover for two main reasons. First, it provides them with protection from predators. Second, it puts them in the best possible position from which to ambush their prey.

Water Quality

Good quality water will support more species of fish and greater populations of fish than polluted and stagnant water, or water lacking adequate oxygen.

Each species of fish occupies its own niche in the ecosystem. However, there is an interdependence among species that must not be ignored. If water conditions change and are no longer suitable for the production of forage species, game fish that rely on that food source will suffer. Their numbers may decline and their growth will be slowed.

Natural events such as heavy rainfalls or a long drought also force changes in water conditions. Fish must either adapt to these changing conditions or move to a new location.

Murky water screens out sunlight and makes photosynthesis more difficult for plants, decreasing oxygen production. Turbidity in the form of silt also settles on the bottom, smothering plants and even the eggs of fish. When the water becomes over-fertilized and polluted, there is usually a serious lack of oxygen.

The introduction of toxic chemicals into the water has an immediate and disastrous effect on fish populations. Each ecosystem is fragile. Natural events and human activities can wipe out a year-class of fish or cause undue stress on the population.

Healthy water conditions support the strongest populations of fish. If pollutants are introduced or habitats destroyed by construction, water quality suffers. This reduces fish populations and, often, the size of individual fish. Fish are extremely sensitive animals that seldom adapt well to rapid change. They require adequate amounts of oxygen and relatively stable water temperatures.

In a marine environment, there are other factors to consider. The amount of salt in the water can be extremely important, especially in estuaries and near-shore ocean waters. Too much fresh water entering these areas from rivers, canals, and water-management areas can easily upset the balance.

Water quality affects fish species differently. Some fish can live in poorer water conditions than others. For example, carp can live in water with higher temperatures and lower oxygen levels than trout could tolerate.

BASIC ECOLOGICAL PRINCIPLES

Survival

Each species finds its place in the web in terms of the foods it eats and the places it can live. Most creatures try to eliminate as much competition as possible through unique adaptations. Those animals that can tolerate and digest a varied diet have a better chance for survival.

As a basic ecological rule, the more tolerant of varying conditions an organism happens to be, the better its chances are for long-term survival. Those creatures that can only exist within a narrow range of conditions are less likely to succeed.

Carrying Capacity

Every body of water, including the oceans, has a **carrying capacity**, which limits the number of living things it can support. Carrying capacity is based on water quality, climate, the shape of the body of water, and the total biomass it is capable of producing and sustaining. Better quality water can support more life. The biomass, or food chain, begins with single-celled algae and ranges through planktonic invertebrates to baitfish and, finally, to the predator species that anglers try to catch.

Bodies of water may contain many small fish or a few large fish. The balance of various species also affects the productivity of each ecosystem. For example:

- If a body of water has a capacity to produce 1000 pounds of fish, there may be 250 four-pound fish or 1,000 one-pound fish.
- In southern regions of the country where the weather is warmer and the growing season is longer, lakes yield greater returns of fish and other aquatic life.

Limiting Factors

If a brand new tire has one small bad spot, that tire is only as good as that weakest spot. The weak spot would be considered a limiting factor.

Any factor that tends to slow down potential growth in an ecosystem is said to be a limiting factor. A particular ecosystem may have good quality water, the right amount of salt, and the right temperature, but lack a particular food source on which a species is dependent. That particular food source would be the limiting factor for that species. For other species, it might be any one of the requirements mentioned in this chapter.

USING ECOLOGICAL PRINCIPLES IN FISHING

A study of food chains demonstrates that waters rich in producers will generate more consumers, especially those of the higher orders. As a first step, anglers should study the waters they fish and try to determine if an abundance of plants, including algae, exists and if they can see significant numbers of small fish or minnows. Without a firm base, the number of **predators** at the top of the food-chain pyramid will be severely limited.

Experienced anglers always feel more comfortable fishing in waters that show an abundance of living things. If you overturn rocks at the shore of a lake and find crayfish, you can be almost certain that there will be bass, particularly smallmouth bass. In contrast, tadpoles in a pond indicate few bass, since the bass would have devoured any available tadpoles. In a trout stream, insect larvae attached to rocks indicate that the water generates plenty of food for trout.

Water that is stagnant, polluted, or otherwise shows signs of having little oxygen will have a much smaller population of fish. You probably will not have much success fishing this kind of water. The key to catching fish is fishing in **productive waters**. It is important to select a body of water where there is a healthy food chain and fish populations are close to the carrying capacity of the waters.

Using food chains as a guide, you will begin to learn the types of food a certain species of fish prefers. Usually, the diet covers a variety of food, but there are primary targets. Whether an angler relies on natural bait or artificial lures, the idea is to give the fish what they want or what they would normally find in those waters. In terms of trout feeding on insects, this is called "matching the hatch," but the idea goes beyond that. If shiners are abundant in a body of water, they would be an excellent bait to use. The same approach goes for menhaden, sardines, pilchards, or other saltwater baitfish. Learn what fish are feeding on and try to offer the same thing or a reasonable imitation.

Because angling effort is aimed at **second-order carnivores**, how they find food is important. Those that ambush their prey will usually be close to some form of cover or use their own coloration to help them blend into the habitat. They wait motionless for their prey to approach and then launch a swift attack. Knowing this, an angler must make sure the bait or lure is worked close to the area where such fish are likely to be because they won't chase their prey a long distance.

In moving water, fish maintain a position where they are shielded from the current. This is particularly true for trout, char, and salmon. When feeding on food carried by the current, they seldom move more than a foot or two to the side to feed. If the bait or lure doesn't drift naturally through this small zone, chances are the fish will ignore it.

Remember that **water temperature** is the most important factor in determining where fish will be if the water contains sufficient oxygen. Even within a body of water, a slight temperature variation can affect the distribution of fish. Look for areas that are a degree or two warmer in cool weather or a little cooler in warm weather. Fish are extremely sensitive and react to such differences.

Along the coasts some species are present during a specific time of the year. They don't arrive until the water temperature is suitable. If that temperature changes dramatically, they leave.

Sometimes, pockets of cold water along the coast will keep a species from migrating northward temporarily and delay the arrival in another area.

Through applying your understanding of the food chain and ecological principles, you will catch more fish. Learn all that you can about the fish you want to catch! Then select a productive area to fish, present your lure or bait skillfully, and HOLD ON TO YOUR ROD!!

ACTIVITIES

Activity 1—Observing Aquatic Life

Your favorite fishing area is a good place to observe aquatic life. Rapidly move a kitchen sieve or fine net through seaweeds or algae close to the shore. Examine the organisms you can see crawling in the vegetation. Often a magnifying glass will let you see some detail on these creatures that can't be seen with the naked eye. If possible, count the number of organisms present. This will be a clue to the health of the area that you fish. If there are numerous small creatures, you can infer that there will be a good supply of larger fish since there is plenty of food at the bottom of the food chain.

Activity 2—Checking Decomposition

Collect some of the ooze from the bottom of a lake or pond. If it has a slight smell, you can conclude that there are decomposers feeding on an abundance of rotting material. If there is too much rotting material, these organisms will use up too much available oxygen and thus suffocate other life in the aquatic community. This situation can happen in home aquariums when the fish are fed too much or too often or in ponds or lakes that receive too many nutrients in the form of fertilizer from nearby yards or fields. Cloudy water and a strong smell indicate an unusual number of decomposers and possible depletion of the oxygen supply.

Activity 3—Adequate Algae

Observe algae or other aquatic plants. Using a garden rake, pull some from the bottom. Prolific growth of aquatic plants may indicate an increase in nutrients. These nutrients could be coming from the runoff from agricultural fields or the leakage of septic systems. In any case, with too many nutrients there will be increased algae growth, followed by decomposition and an increase in decomposers. Since decomposers utilize oxygen, this cycle would create a severe reduction in dissolved oxygen which, in turn, would limit some species from living in this environment and in other cases would limit the fish populations.

Activity 4—How Water Temperature Affects Fish

Materials: 1 fish and 1 tank or bowl

Place the fish in water at room temperature. After several minutes (10 is plenty), observe the movement of the gill covers. Count the movements for two minutes. Do this 5 times, and find the average per minute. Next place several ice cubes in the water and wait for the temperature to drop. (Use enough ice so that the temperature drop is noticeable). Repeat your observations and compare the two averages. Was the average higher or lower in the colder water? Do you know why? Does this give you any hint about fish movement or activity as winter comes to a pond?

CHAPTER 13

FISH BEHAVIOR

WHY FISH BEHAVE THE WAY THEY DO

Learning why fish act the way they do is both interesting and important. Once you understand their behavior, you will appreciate fish and their role in nature. You can then use this information to know where and how to fish.

Behavior is nothing more than the unique reaction an animal exhibits as it interacts with its environment. In previous chapters you have learned about a fish's senses, preferred water temperature and water type, food and oxygen requirements, and its position in the predator-prey food chain. All of these factors affect the behavior of fish. Other factors that affect behavior include body characteristics, seasonal changes, migration, reproduction, growth, and feeding patterns.

THE SHAPE OF FISH

Shape of the Body

The body shape of a fish controls what it does, how it moves, and what it eats. For example, northern pike and barracuda have long slender bodies. They are able to lunge ahead quickly to strike at a small fish or at a lure. They can't, however, turn as quickly as bass or bluegill to catch food or chase your lure or bait.

Fish come in many shapes and this shape controls the speed at which they can swim. Some fish are long and narrow; some are short and thick-bodied. For example, a trout that spends most of its life in a river's flowing water has a more streamlined body than a largemouth bass that lives among the weeds of a lake. The trout's body is sleek so that flowing water passes around it easily. It also has a wide, powerful tail that gives it great speed. A bass has a chunkier body and a broad, flat tail that provides greater maneuverability in dense weeds. Larger fish are usually able to swim faster, but they are less maneuverable.

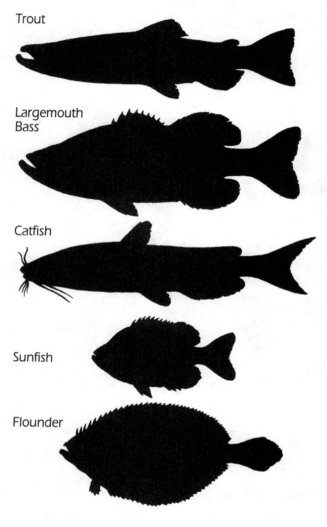

Trout

Largemouth Bass

Catfish

Sunfish

Flounder

Fish Shapes

Shape and Location of the Mouth

You can also learn much about a species by looking at the shape and location of its mouth. The sharp, pointy teeth of fish like the muskellunge, walleye, sea trout, and bluefish are good for catching and holding slippery fish. The mouth of fish like the sucker, sturgeon, bonefish, carp, and cod makes them ideal bottom-feeders. Bottom-feeders move frequently in search of food, while predators often prefer to wait and ambush passing food.

SEASONS AND MOVEMENT

Migration. A good angler must learn about fish migration. Some species migrate or move on a daily basis. These include movements from shallow to deep water or from deep to shallow water, movement into feeding areas, and movement that varies with the light intensity or water temperature. During the warmer months, many species spend more time in the shallows to search for food. Often, as light intensity increases, they move out of the unprotected shallows where they could become prey for birds or shoreline animals and migrate to protected deeper waters. Even if not searching for food in the shallows, many species are sensitive to bright light and move to deep waters for this reason.

Seasons. Different seasons find fish in different places and exhibiting different behavior. Anglers must adjust to these variations to catch fish consistently. During the year there are changes in water temperature, the amount of light and the number of hours of daylight. In summer there is more light and more hours of sunlight than during the winter. When light increases, fish such as flounder and bass move out of the unprotected shallows and move to deeper waters. When water temperatures are lower during the winter months in northern areas, the activity of fish slows down and they eat less food. When water warms in the spring, most fish return to shallower waters, begin spawning, and feed more often. Anglers call this cycle a "seasonal pattern." Species of fish can be counted on to repeat this pattern year after year. Anglers use this type of information to become more successful.

A saltwater fish's movements are based on season, tides, currents resulting from tidal flows, and movement of its prey. Bluefish found in Florida in the winter may be found in Maine during the following summer. Similarly, tuna "wintering" in Mexico may visit Canada in the summer!

FISH REPRODUCTION

To an angler, spawning of fish is more than a means of reproducing a species. Usually there is a movement, or migration, associated with spawning as well as changes in behavior. What a fish does at such

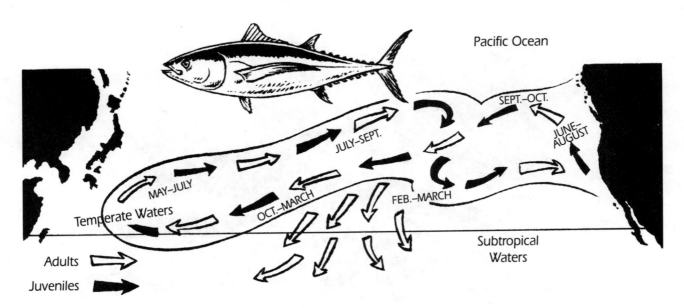

Pacific Ocean

SEPT.–OCT.

JUNE–AUGUST

JULY–SEPT.

MAY–JULY

Temperate Waters

OCT.–MARCH

FEB.–MARCH

Subtropical Waters

Adults

Juveniles

Albacore Tuna Migration

times can be broken down into three periods—the time just before it spawns **(pre-spawn period)**, spawning **(spawn period)**, and the time just after spawning **(post-spawn period)**. Knowing what occurs during each of these periods is important to a successful catch.

Spawning Cycles as Behavior Regulators

The biological urge to spawn overrides other more typical behavioral patterns of fish. Reproduction is vital for the continued survival of each species. Reproduction usually follows three basic methods.

Methods of Reproduction. The female of most species deposits its eggs in the water. The eggs are then immediately fertilized by sperm from the male. After a period of time, the eggs hatch. Fish that produce eggs which hatch outside the body are called **oviparous.**

By another method, the eggs are fertilized while they are still inside the female's body. Then they are deposited in the water and, after a certain time, hatch.

A third method also involves fertilizing the eggs while they are still inside the female's body, but the young, or fry, are born alive. This method is used by guppies, sun perch, mosquitofish, rays, and some sharks. Fish that produce living young are called **viviparous**.

A fish must be sexually mature to spawn. The age at maturity varies among species. The shorter time a species lives, the sooner it reaches sexual maturity. Species such as bass and trout tend to spawn every year once they are mature. Salmon, however, require two to five years before they spawn and then most salmon species die soon after spawning. Some eels may only spawn once every 10 to 12 years.

All fish do not spawn at the same time or deposit all of their eggs at one time. If all the fish in a lake were to deposit eggs on the same day, a sudden severe drop in water temperature could destroy all of the eggs.

Spawning Locations. Each species prefers a specific kind of habitat for spawning. During the pre-spawn period, a fish begins to change its pattern of behavior and moves into position to get ready for the actual spawn. This pre-spawn movement can be slight, such as when bass and bluegill select a nearby site for a spawning bed. However, stream trout make a significant movement when they leave their preferred feeding territory and move to a stream's headwaters or up a tributary of the stream to spawn.

Mature Pacific salmon leave the ocean and ascend a river until they reach the location where they were born. They accomplish this by using their keen sense of smell. When they were young, the salmon received a chemical imprint of the water and use that information to return. Spawning salmon swim

Fish Spawning

over small waterfalls and up manmade fish ladders and other obstacles until they arrive at the spawning site to build a **redd**, or nest.

Striped bass also come in from the sea to spawn, but they try to find brackish water with the proper amount of salinity to hold their free-floating eggs in suspension until they hatch.

In contrast to Pacific salmon and striped bass, the American eel lives in fresh water and spawns in salt water. These eels leave coastal rivers and make their way to the Sargasso Sea near Bermuda where reproduction occurs. Then, the young eels must find their way back to the rivers.

Fish that are ready to spawn are heavier because of the roe, or eggs, in females and the milt, or sperm, in males. The eggs in a female may account for as much as 25% or more of its body weight, while the milt in the male could account for about 12% of its body weight.

Breeding. Breeding takes place in several ways, depending on the species. Some fish gather in large schools when it is time to spawn. Others gather in smaller groups. One female may spawn with several males. Tarpon have a ritual of forming a circle and swimming around and around. Some species pair off, frequently building a nest to hold the eggs.

The female **salmon** digs a redd with its powerful tail while the male guards the nest, driving away other fish. Then, the female settles over the redd and the male swims over, touching her dorsal fin or nudging her body with his snout. When it is time to spawn, he curves his body around hers. As she deposits the eggs, he fertilizes them immediately.

Bass and other members of the **sunfish** family build nests. The largemouth bass builds a nest close to shore where the young will have some form of protective cover. The fertilized eggs drop to the bottom of the nest and adhere, while the male bass stands guard and fans them constantly to keep silt from settling on them. Bass will not feed while guarding the nest, but they will use their mouth to move anything away from the eggs or the fry. That is why a bass will strike lures at this time. Eventually, the young fry are abandoned by the male and left to fend for themselves. Spawning takes place in the spring and seems to be triggered by water temperature ranging from 60 to 70 degrees F.

The **bluegill** spawns a little later, preferring a water temperature of about 70 degrees F. Like the bass, the bluegill builds a nest in the shallows.

The **crappie** also spawns in shallow water, but likes to build its nest near vegetation and waits until late spring or early summer to spawn. The crappie has a similar nest-guarding behavior. A single female crappie may deposit 150,000 eggs in the nest; however, most of the juveniles are eaten by the parents.

The **brown** and **brook trout** spawn in the fall, but the native rainbow and cutthroat trout spawn in the early spring. **Trout, salmon**, and **walleye** deposit their eggs over gravel bars where there is a good flow of water to prevent silt from covering them. The colder the water, the longer it takes for

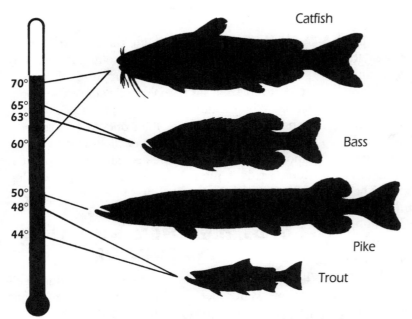

Catfish

Bass

Pike

Trout

70°
65°
63°
60°
50°
48°
44°

Fish Spawn in Water of Different Temperature

fry must feed on their own. They are then considered to be juveniles until they reach sexual maturity.

For anglers, knowing the time of year that various species spawn and where they go during this period is necessary for successful fishing. An angler has to make an informed decision on whether removing spawning fish will affect the population in that body of water.

Sexual Differences—Dimorphism

In most species of fish, you cannot tell male from female just by looking at the fish. However, there are exceptions. For example, the male, or bull dolphin, has a blunt forehead; the female has a rounded head. Males of some catfish species have longer barbels than the females. In some flounder species, the male has longer pectoral or dorsal fins.

Physical Changes During the Spawn. During spawning or just prior to it, some species undergo changes that make it easier to tell male from female. Large, mature salmon and trout males commonly develop a kype, or hook, on the lower jaw and sometimes one on the upper jaw. At this time, the male salmon may also develop a dorsal hump. The males of a few minnow and sucker species become covered with horny breeding tubercles that help them drive away other males.

eggs to hatch. Trout eggs often take two to three months or even longer to hatch, and all the eggs do not hatch at the same time. Salmon and trout eggs and the young fry are vulnerable to predators.

Fish that build nests, which require greater parental care, usually deposit fewer eggs than those that broadcast, or spread, their eggs at random. For example, bass and sunfish may only deposit a few hundred eggs, while the average cod may deposit as many as three million eggs.

Those species of fish that spread their eggs in open water offer no parental protection or care of the young. They simply deposit the eggs, fertilize them, and let nature take its course. Of the millions of eggs released, enough survive to repeat the cycle for another generation.

Once eggs are deposited and fertilized, cell division begins. The embryo gets its nourishment from the egg's yolk sac. Development of the larvae is usually rapid and takes from a few hours to several days. Once the yolk sac is exhausted, the tiny

Spawning Over a Gravel Bar

Coloration among males and females is much the same except at spawning time. Individual fish may have darker or lighter shades, depending on their habitat, but there is little difference between the sexes until spawning time. Just before spawning, male trout and salmon have more intense coloration than the females.

When Pacific salmon begin returning from the sea to spawn, they are firm, powerful fish with bright silver coloration and a dark back. Once they enter a river, they no longer feed, at least not regularly, but live off fat and protein stored in their bodies. Their main goal is to reach the location of their birth and spawn. Soon afterward they die. Some Atlantic salmon, however, do survive after spawning and return to the sea. At spawning time, the coloration of Pacific salmon changes; they become much darker, and the flesh of once-firm bodies deteriorates.

After dying, the rotting carcasses of salmon provide food for a variety of birds and animals and, more importantly, put nutrients back into the rivers. These nutrients support aquatic life that sustains the salmon fry and juveniles during the next year. If these salmon did not die after spawning, there would not be enough food in the streams and rivers to feed the young.

Size. In many species the female grows much larger than the male. This is certainly true for largemouth bass, striped bass, walleye, marlin, and tarpon. When an angler catches a particularly large fish, chances are it is a female. The opposite, however, is true for dolphin; males grow larger than the females.

Importance of Spawning Cycles

Several species of salmon may use the same river system to spawn, but not at the same time. There may be more than one spawning run in a given year. This separates the spawns so that each species has the area to itself.

Nature is a complex phenomenon in which interdependence is often critical. A game fish may spawn before a certain baitfish species that later is an important part of its diet. In that way, the predator is slightly larger than its prey and is able to eat it. Without this food, the predator's fry would not survive.

In salt water, spawning often takes place during a season that coincides with certain tides or currents. Flying fish spawn when the Sargassum weed is present. The eggs of this species resemble tiny berry-like floats that support the weed. This camouflages the eggs and gives the fry a place to hide and grow.

With all of the perils facing the eggs and subsequent fry, the odds seem insurmountable that any ever grow into adult fish. Each mature adult must at least replace itself to maintain a stable fish population. When additional fish are produced, populations rise. Anything less than one-for-one replacement results in a population decline. However, the amount of fishing pressure also affects fish populations, as do a number of other factors, including pollution and the destruction of habitat.

FOODS, DIGESTION, NUTRITION, AND GROWTH

To survive and eventually spawn, a fish must feed and grow. Its diet and habitat play an important part in its growth, as well as how quickly it can convert food into energy and weight.

Fish and the Food Network

To feed and grow well, a fish not only needs food, but also must assimilate that food into its system efficiently. As food enters the bloodstream of a fish, it is first used to supply energy for internal functions and its immediate activities. Anything left over then goes toward building muscle, tissue, and bone. Some excess food can be stored for later use in the form of fat, but that takes place only after the first two needs have been fulfilled.

Most fish must consume daily amounts of average quality food, equal to about one-percent of their body weight, just to stay alive and active. That means a three-pound bass has to eat about half an ounce of food every day, almost 11.5 pounds of food a year, just to survive.

A fish uses a considerable amount of energy when feeding heavily. Therefore, feeding frenzies are usually over quickly. A school of predators may attack baitfish, feed briefly, and then return to a normal swimming pace to rest. It is also important to recognize that fish often feed when there is an opportunity.

Within any body of water, the relationship of a predator to its prey is extremely complex. Most game fish will eat almost any kind of smaller fish, including its own kind. By doing so, the predator limits the numbers of its prey and controls that species. Baitfish usually live shorter lives than game fish and reproduce more quickly. If there isn't enough food

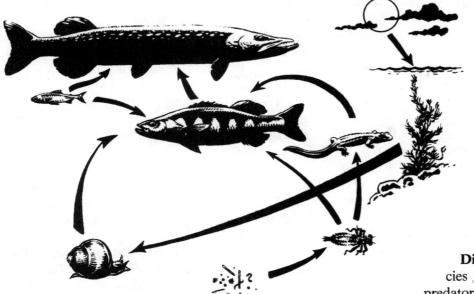

A Food Web

for predators, they go elsewhere or their numbers decline, giving the prey population a chance to recover. A shortage of food affects the growth of a predator and often reduces the rate of reproduction. An abundance of food causes rapid growth and much greater reproduction.

At times, a species will focus on one type of prey, ignoring others. As a general rule, fish tend to take the largest prey that they can swallow easily. This gives them a greater return for the effort expended. They also select and attack one victim at a time. If a prey becomes isolated, disabled, or looks different than the others, it is more likely to be singled out and attacked by a predator. When baitfish school they present a shimmering mass to a predator, making it difficult for the predator to isolate its prey. Baitfish that stray from the school are often picked off easily.

Food Conversion and Nutrition

Digestion. Even under ideal conditions, fish need at least 12 hours to digest and assimilate food, but this can vary due to many factors. This chemical process depends on body temperature. Because fish are cold-blooded creatures, the temperature of the water determines how fast their food will be digested. How much a fish has in its stomach has little bearing on the time required for digestion.

For example, a largemouth bass living in 72-degree F water would need about 18 hours to digest the food in its stomach. That same task would take

almost four days during winter in the northern part of the country. The colder the water, the less food a fish requires. Therefore, it would need to feed only every four or five days in cold weather.

Experts believe that swordfish come to the surface of the ocean during the middle of the day to benefit from warmer water temperatures to help with digestion.

Diet and Nutrition. Most species rely on a varied diet, but a predator may concentrate on a certain type of prey if it is abundant. Fish also seem to prefer the foods that give them the most energy.

In fresh water, the crayfish is a favorite food just as the shrimp is in salt water. Studies show that fish that feed mainly on crayfish grow much faster than those that prefer other prey. When crayfish are abundant, they become a favorite food and other prey become secondary. A body of water with a large crayfish population frequently produces more than its share of trophy-size fish.

During a Minnesota study, bass were put in a pond with 1,000 crayfish and 1,000 bluegills. At the end of 20 days, the bass had eaten 24 crayfish for every bluegill. More importantly, those bass on a bluegill diet lost weight while those that fed on crayfish gained weight.

In salt water, crabs, shrimp, and other crustacea seem to produce similar growth patterns. Perhaps it is easier for a game fish to catch crustacea than baitfish.

Fish Growth

A number of factors determine how fast a fish will grow, including the abundance of food as well as the temperature and condition of the water.

Each species has a typical lifespan. Baitfish, like minnows, may only live a year, while a trout may live for six to eight years or more. The longer the average life of a fish, the more time it takes to grow and reach sexual maturity. There are many 100-pound tarpon, but it takes them nearly 12 years to reach that size. A dolphin, however, may only live four or five years and reaches its maximum size and weight in that time.

Theoretically, a fish is capable of growth throughout its life, but most growth occurs in the early years. A study of bluegills showed that two-year-old fish were able to assimilate a little over 30 percent of the protein they ate, but eight-year-old bluegills could barely convert 20%. Also, younger fish often put three times as much food value to work in growth than an older fish. A trophy fish does not put on weight very easily even though it can stalk larger prey and may feed heavily.

Age and growth information of fish populations is necessary for successful fisheries management and conservation. The goal is to insure that enough fish live long enough to maintain reproduction. Because sexual maturity in some species is not reached for several years, these fish must be protected longer. Fast-growing, short-lived species can be caught and kept at a younger age.

FEEDING HABITS OF FISH

Many species of fish seldom roam far from the spot where they were born. It is common for trout to live most of their lives in one small section of stream. Even when they move for the winter or to spawn, they return to that exact place the next season. Fish cannot know that food may be more plentiful upstream or downstream or on the other side of a lake. They tend to stay in one small location, regardless of the food supply.

Pelagic ocean fish live differently, moving about all the time. Water temperature, currents, and the availability of prey influences their movements. Frequently, game fish follow baitfish migrations, feeding on the prey for a considerable distance.

Water depth is often a key to finding certain species. If sailfish are found in 120 feet of water at one spot, other sailfish will be at that depth a considerable distance away. No one knows why, but it happens regularly.

When migratory tarpon appear in the Florida Keys in spring, they move from the backcountry side of the Keys to the ocean side. No one can predict the exact day this occurs, but most of the fish move at the same time.

Each species has its own feeding behavior. Fish use a considerable amount of energy to find food. To save energy, some fish hide and wait for food to come by, while other fish constantly hunt. The largemouth bass, northern pike, and muskellunge are "ambush" feeders; they prefer to hide or remain stationary, waiting for the prey to come within range, and then strike. Young bass may chase prey a considerable distance, but mature bass seldom do.

Trout anglers talk about **feeding lanes** in a stream where food is carried to fish by the current. Research has shown that there are certain spots, known best to trout, where they feed. If one fish leaves this area, another fish takes its place.

Over time, each fish species has worked out a survival strategy from which it seldom deviates. That is the lifestyle of the species and young and old live it together. Anglers study and learn these behavior patterns of fish. Anglers have a better chance of success once they understand how fish feed and know the habitat fish occupy.

An Ambush Feeder

ACTIVITIES

Activity 1—What Do Fish Eat?

You can determine the current food of a particular species by examining the contents of the stomach. While dressing your catch, open the stomach and examine the contents. If there are numerous "shell" parts, they could be the exoskeletons of insects. Often parts of smaller fish will be observed. These clues help you to understand the predator-prey relationship. In addition, you can use this information to determine the type of bait or lure to use while you are fishing.

Activity 2—Locating Fish Nests

In the spring of the year, visit a local lake or pond and walk around the banks. Look into the shallow water and try to see fish nests where they lay their eggs. These "nests" will appear to be light colored areas on the lake bottom and look like the fish swept the area clear of debris. If you look carefully, you may even see the fish "on the nest."

WATER AS AN ENVIRONMENT

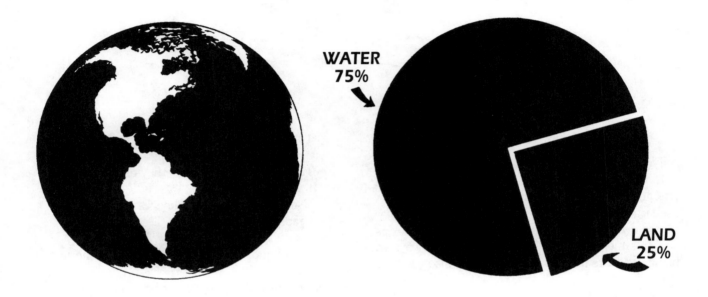

WATER 75%

LAND 25%

Good anglers are concerned about the fish's primary need—WATER. You probably don't think much about water even though you use it every day. Water is very important because there's nothing else like it in the world. Next to the air we breathe, water is probably the most important thing in our lives. Fish are not the only animals that could not live without it. We couldn't live without it either and can't afford to take it for granted.

There is a great deal of water, covering about 70 percent of the earth, but only about three percent of it is fresh water. Most of this fresh water, about 75 percent, is in the form of ice. In fact, the frozen areas of the world have as much fresh water as all the world's rivers will carry for the next 1,000 years.

The demand for unpolluted fresh water is increasing because the earth's population is increasing. How much water does the average person use? Here are some answers:

- **In the home, each person uses about 70 gallons of water a day.**
- **It takes three gallons to flush a toilet.**
- **It takes 15 to 30 gallons to take a bath.**
- **It takes five gallons for a one-minute shower.**
- **It takes 10 gallons to wash dishes.**

This is a lot of water, but more than half of the water used in the United States is used by industry. For example, it takes 250 tons of water to make a ton of newspaper and ten gallons to produce one gallon of gasoline. You can see why it is important to conserve water.

Water Has Multiple Uses

SHARING WATERS

As you have seen, anglers and boaters are not the only ones who use bodies of water and have an effect on fish populations. Industries and power plants use large amounts of water. Communities need water for drinking. Farmers use it to water their crops and livestock. Barges and ships use waterways to bring products to market and water is also used for waste disposal.

The demands for water use can cause conflicts among those using water resources. The results are not always good for the fish but not everyone is concerned with fish.

An occasional conflict arises when people want to dam a river for irrigation, for controlling floods, or for the production of electricity. Dams create lakes or reservoirs that are habitat for fish such as largemouth bass and crappie. However, the reservoir can destroy several miles of river that are prime habitat for trout, smallmouth, or rock bass.

Water is too valuable to waste. With so much demand for water, it is important that each of us do our part by:

- Reducing water use in the kitchen and bathroom.
- Shutting the water off between rinsing dishes or brushing our teeth.

- Turning the water on only when we are actually using it.
- Taking showers because they use less water than baths.
- Using flow-restricting devices on shower heads.
- Fixing leaky faucets.
- Running only full loads of clothes in the washer.
- Placing a plastic bottle or brick in the water tank of the toilet so that it will use less water for each flushing.
- Not using water for watering lawns or washing cars during times of water shortage.

THE NATURE OF WATER

Physical and Chemical Features

Liquid, Gas, and Solid. Two hydrogen atoms and one oxygen atom combine as a molecule to form water. Water turns into ice at a temperature of 32 degrees F, 0 degrees C, and boils at 212 degrees F, 100 degrees C. No other substance can accomplish that within that temperature span. Between those temperatures, water is a liquid; below those temperatures it is a solid—ice; and above those temperatures it is a gas—vapor.

Turnover

Water also has the ability to store a large amount of heat. This is important to remember because it means that water warms and cools more slowly than land or air. This brings a moderating influence to land masses near large bodies of water, keeping them cooler in the summer and warmer in the winter than would otherwise be possible by location alone.

Surface Tension

Surface tension is the ability of a substance to stick to itself and pull itself together. Water has a high surface tension that forms a film on the water's surface. Small organisms live on top or just underneath this film. This surface tension can be so strong that when some organisms break through in either direction, they cannot get back.

Water as a Solvent

Water is often called the **universal solvent**. This is because water can dissolve so many things, some such as salt and sugar, very quickly. Other materials may take thousands or even millions of years to dissolve. For example, flowing water can dissolve rock. That, along with other types of erosion, is how the Grand Canyon and other canyons and river valleys were formed.

Density

Cold water is more dense and heavier than warm water. Water continues to get heavier until it reaches a temperature of 39.2 degrees F. At this temperature, one cubic foot of water weighs more than 62 pounds. Then something unusual happens. Water colder than 39 degrees F begins to get lighter or less dense. As water turns into ice it adds about nine percent to its volume, enabling ice to float. No other liquid acts this way.

What does this mean to an angler? Well, if water colder than 39 degrees F did not get lighter, ice wouldn't float. Instead, ice would form on the bottom of a lake and kill the fish and other aquatic life.

The Turnover

As the sun melts ice on a northern lake in spring and begins to heat the surface water, a change takes place. When the surface water reaches about 39 degrees F, it begins to sink to the bottom, helped by wind and currents. This pushes colder water on the bottom toward the surface. Anglers call this mixing of water **the turnover**. The turnover occurs twice— once in the spring and again in the fall.

After the turnover, the water temperature of the mixed water is nearly the same throughout the lake. During these periods, fish are likely to be scattered and at any depth.

Water Layers

In summer, something occurs on many deep or large lakes. The water forms into three layers, each with a different range of temperature. The sun warms the top layer **(epilimnion)** faster than the wind can mix it. Another layer **(hypolimnion)** is the heavy cold water at the bottom of the lake. This layer has little oxygen. The third layer is a narrow one that

Water Layers

separates the top and bottom layers, called the **metalimnion,** and contains a **thermocline.** The water temperature in this layer changes rapidly with only small changes in depth.

Why is knowing about these layers important? One reason is that the bottom layer in some lakes has little oxygen. This forces fish to move to a higher level and into the metalimnion, near the thermocline. So, in summer on lakes that separate into layers, fish will frequently move to the epilimnion to feed and then return to their preferred temperatures near the thermocline.

Freshwater lakes are not the only places where water forms into layers. This also occurs in saltwater estuaries and in the oceans.

Viscosity

Because water is viscous, thick like syrup or glue, it offers resistance to aquatic animals that they must overcome by an expenditure of energy. A trade-off occurs because a body placed in water seems to become lighter. A force equal to the weight of the displaced water buoys up the body. This also allows a fish and other animals to maintain buoyancy and counters the tendency to sink. Salt water is more dense, and therefore, more buoyant, than fresh water.

To the human eye, all water looks the same. Actually, water changes in viscosity as its temperature changes. Water is twice as viscous at 32 degrees F as it is at 86 degrees F. This change can be demonstrated by pouring a glass of ice water into a sink and then pouring some boiling water from a kettle in the sink. The boiling water will splash much more

than the cold water, showing that the cold water is much more viscous.

Transparency and Absorption of Color in Water

Water clarity controls the amount of light that can penetrate the water and the depth to which it penetrates. Under extremely clear conditions, almost all light is filtered out within the first 30 feet. This means that if you can't see a lure 30 feet deep when looking vertically, you can't see it 30 feet away if you are under water viewing it horizontally. However, in a muddy lake or river, it may be totally dark only a few feet below the surface.

It is important to remember that light is the essential ingredient in photosynthesis, explaining why plant growth is limited to relatively shallow water. Plankton and silt particles can cause turbidity, which limits light penetration. This has tremendous implications for a body of water and its ability to support plants providing the food chain necessary for fish populations.

When we look at something, we see it in terms of the light rays reflected from it. These light rays travel in waves. Our eyes see colors because each color is represented by a different wavelength. Darkness and loss of color increases with depth. Colors with long wavelengths are absorbed quickly. The red end of the light spectrum disappears in less than 30 feet of clear water, less than that when the water is turbid. Blues and greens have shorter wavelengths and are the slowest to be absorbed.

Because of the different wavelengths of light, colors appear differently at greater depths. Blues and greens are visible at depths where red objects, whose color has been absorbed, appear to be black.

Fluorescent colors retain their hues deeper than standard colors. Orange, which is close to red in the spectrum, seems to keep its color much deeper, but not as deep as blue, green, and even yellow.

Some anglers give lure color a low priority when selecting a lure. They believe that approach, presentation of the lure, and the retrieve are more important than color. They may begin with a dark-colored lure and, if that doesn't work, switch to a light-colored lure, or the opposite. Some research, however, indicates that lure color may be more important than previously believed. Today, many companies are producing lures with colors identified by electronic instruments.

The Water Cycle

The heat from the sun causes water on the earth to evaporate, or turn into a vapor, and rise into the atmosphere. Sooner or later, the water falls to earth in the form of rain or snow. When water strikes the earth, some of it turns to vapor through evaporation, and some of it enters brooks, creeks, streams and rivers. Eventually this water makes its way into the oceans. Water also seeps into the ground, becoming groundwater. It moves slowly until it reaches rivers and lakes or drains into large underground areas called aquifers. As the cycle repeats itself, all of the water returns to earth and none is lost.

WATER MANAGEMENT

The bad news is that there is a limited amount of water in the world. In fact, there's no more water today than there was when the earth was formed. The good news is that water is recycled. Over time, it is used over and over again. Because of this, it's important not to pollute water so that it cannot be used safely by humans, fish, and other life forms that depend on it for survival.

If water is kept pure and used wisely, there will be enough for our needs. Some areas, like those around the Great Lakes, have more fresh water than others. However, states in the Southwest must bring in water from other places.

We need to make sure that we keep our waters clean and free from pollution. The quality of water is very important for fish and other animals to live and thrive.

When harmful things enter our waters, they become polluted. Polluted water cannot be used for drinking, swimming, or fishing. The key lies in eliminating pollution. Fortunately, you can make a difference! In chapter 16 you will learn about different types of pollution. You will also learn how you can become part of the solution instead of part of the problem.

If water is kept clean and used wisely, there will be enough for our many needs.

The Water Cycle

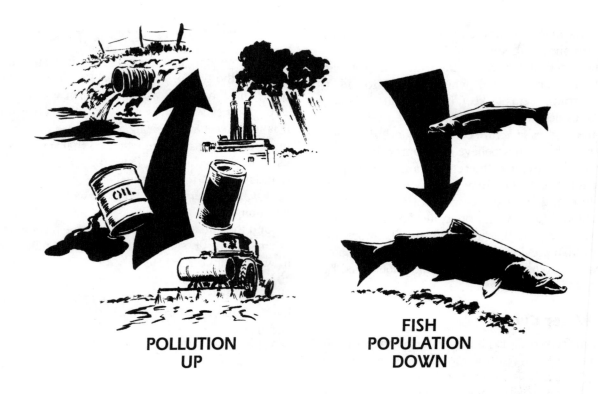

POLLUTION
UP

FISH
POPULATION
DOWN

ACTIVITIES

Activity 1—Buoyancy

Put 1 1/2 cups of water in a glass two-cup measure. Now put an egg in the water (be careful not to break it). What happened to the egg? Remove the egg. Add 1/2 cup of table salt and stir to dissolve as much as possible. Replace the egg and observe what happens.

Things float because of upward pressure by the water they displace. This is called buoyancy. As you observed, the egg floated in salt water. This indicates that salt water has more buoyancy than fresh water. This is because salt water has a greater density than fresh water. Do you see that it would be easier to swim in the ocean than in fresh water?

It has been said that it is nearly impossible to drown in the Dead Sea. Why might this be true?

Activity 2—Creating A Water Cycle

Since there is very little water being produced in this world, we must live with that which is here now. That means that it must be recycled. Nature's recycling is called the water cycle. If you want to explain this phenomenon, try this.

Put a pan of water on the stove. (This will be your ocean or lake). Turn on the stove to heat the water (the heat represents the sun). Evaporation occurs as the water heats. In evaporation, liquid water changes to a vapor or invisible gas in the air. Now put some ice cubes in a glass and hold the glass above the water. Water droplets will collect on the outside of the glass. This is because condensation occurs, changing the gas back into a liquid. As the water collects, some of it will drip back into the pan and represents rain. Thus the water cycle is complete.

Activity 3—Watching Turnover

Fill a 9" x 13" pyrex or other glass, heat resistant dish with water. At one end place a small plastic bag filled with ice. Carefully add some boiling water in the end opposite the bag of ice. Place several drops of green or blue food coloring next to the bag of ice. Watch where the drop of dye goes. What happens to the dye when it reaches the warm end of the dish? The dye sinks at the cold end and moves to the warm end where it rises and begins its drift back to the cold end. In the Spring, cold water in lakes sinks and the warm water moves to the surface. The opposite happens in the fall.

CHAPTER 15

AQUATIC COMMUNITIES

Each species of fish prefers a certain habitat. Habitat is where a fish lives and must contain adequate oxygen, tolerable temperature, adequate food, space and hiding places (cover). A variety of aquatic communities can fulfill these needs for different fish.

FRESHWATER LAKES AND PONDS

Many lakes were formed thousands of years ago by glaciers, massive "rivers" of ice, that carved valleys and depressions in the earth. These valleys and depressions were filled with melting water from the glaciers and became lakes. In recent times, dams built to block the flow of rivers have also formed lakes, often called reservoirs or impoundments.

Ponds are tiny lakes and many are shaped like a bowl. Many farm ponds are used to store rainwater for crops or livestock. They are often great places to fish!

Features of Lakes and Ponds

The Water's Surface. Since many tiny organisms, called **neuston,** live on the water's surface on lakes and ponds, if you look closely, you may be able to see these dust-size creatures.

For some species of fish, the surface is an excellent feeding area. Species such as bass, bluegill and trout often eat insects that fall on the water. Anything that makes a disturbance on the water's surface attracts the attention of fish. If the water is

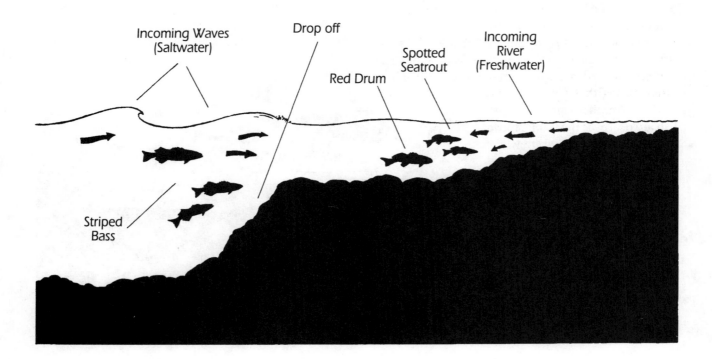

Incoming Waves (Saltwater)   Drop off   Red Drum   Spotted Seatrout   Incoming River (Freshwater)

Striped Bass

Surface as a Feeding Area

shallow and the sun is shining, the shadow of anything on the surface generally appears on the bottom. This, too, will alert fish to a possible feeding opportunity.

The Pelagic Zone. Fish that spend a considerable amount of time in open water are called **pelagic** species. Striped bass stocked in freshwater impoundments fall into this category as well as Pacific salmon stocked in the Great Lakes. Both prefer the open water and follow their food supply.

Plankton are tiny plants (**phytoplankton**) and animals (**zooplankton**) in the water. Small fish roam open areas of a lake and feed on zooplankton. Larger fish often follow and feed on these small fish.

Large predator fish usually lurk below the small fish, forcing them toward the surface. Whenever you see small fish on the surface in open water, it often means that larger fish are feeding. Another sign that larger fish are nearby is the frantic movement of small fish that may even jump out of the water while trying to escape.

The Littoral Zone. The shallow area along a shoreline is called the **littoral zone** and is critical to the growth of rooted plants. In many cases, sunlight penetrates the water all the way to the bottom, making it possible for many different kinds of plants to grow and thrive. Such emergent plants include cattails, rushes, lilies, pondweed, and marsh grasses.

Plants with floating leaves, such as lilies and pondweed, grow in water to about 10 feet deep. They can be identified by their slender, flexible stems and leaves that float on the surface. There also are rootless, floating plants, such as water hyacinth and duckweed, that live on the surface of the water.

Submerged rooted species that have the ability to absorb carbon dioxide directly from the water and give off oxygen make up another group of aquatic vegetation. Some examples are milfoil and hornwort.

These aquatic plants are important because they produce the oxygen that fish need to live, but too much vegetation makes fishing difficult. Large amounts of dead and decaying plant life also consumes considerable oxygen.

The littoral zone is a haven for both small and large fish. Small fish, like bluegill, feed and hide in plants, brush piles, and logs. Larger predators, like northern pike, come to feed on the smaller fish and also to spawn. Northern pike and bass wait to ambush their prey among the weeds.

Large fish frequently invade the littoral zone during periods of low-light levels. That's why early morning and evening are some of the best times to fish shallow areas.

The Bottom. The bottom of any body of water is a home for many types of aquatic life. Lake bottoms are divided into the shallow littoral zone and the **profundal**, a deep-water zone beyond the littoral. The profundal represents the deep part of the lake and refers to waters where there is little light, low oxygen content, and a relatively high level of carbon dioxide.

Decomposers are found on the bottom. It is important to remember that the process of decomposition uses oxygen, and there may be little oxygen near the bottom at certain times of the year. Animals on or near the bottom feed on decomposers. These include larval forms of insects like stoneflies, several types of worms, and some species of fish like darters. The bottom attracts many fish because it offers an excellent hiding place, has little current, and has more stable temperatures than the surface.

For anglers, the type of bottom is important. Frequently fish will stay on an edge where the bottom changes, for example, from sand to gravel or from mud to sand. Also, any objects on the bottom, such as rocks and logs, or features such as holes or elevations, often attract fish.

FRESHWATER RIVERS AND STREAMS

Flowing rivers and streams are constantly changing. The shape of a river bed controls the amount of water and sediment (sand, rock and soil) a river can carry. During or after a heavy rainfall, the water level and the speed of a current can increase quickly. The water level in a river can also drop quickly in dry weather and become only a series of pools. These conditions force fish and other creatures to adjust to a variety of conditions if they are to live.

Features of Rivers and Streams

The River Banks. In a straight stretch of river, the main force of the current is in the middle. The deepest water is also in the middle and the area near the shore is the shallowest. When there's a sharp bend in the river, however, the strongest current and deepest water is at the outside edge of the bend. Some anglers believe that most fish are in the deeper parts of moving water. That, however, isn't necessarily true. Trout, for example, may station themselves over a gravel bar near shore.

Deep Water. In flowing water, there is less current near the bottom. Because of this, most fish stay with their bellies almost touching the bottom. They like to take advantage of low spots that have even less current than the surrounding water. They do this to save their energy and to avoid being pushed downstream.

Most fish in a river face the flow of water and wait for food to come to them. Trout and salmon like cold, moving water. They will usually stay near the edge of the current and eat whatever food comes along. At night or when light levels are low, the fish often move to shallow water to feed.

It's important to understand that fish in current seldom move far for food. An angler must present a bait or lure accurately or it will be carried downstream without a strike. Fish feeding in a current have only a second or two to decide whether or not to take an offering.

Rainbow trout prefer locations near fast water and take up positions alongside riffles, but they are seldom in the main current. They can be found on the edges and down toward the tail of the run as it starts to smooth out.

The tail end of a pool ranks high as a feeding area for fish because the water is moving slower. Depth decreases in this area because of siltation. Fish have a habit of favoring such locations.

Fish Locations in Flowing Water

ESTUARIES

An estuary is the wide lower course of a river where the ocean's salty water mixes with the fresh water of rivers or streams. An ocean tide brings in salt water and carries out some fresh water when it recedes. As the waters mix, the water with the most salt is near the bottom because it is heavier. The brackish water—the water with less salt—is near the surface because it is lighter.

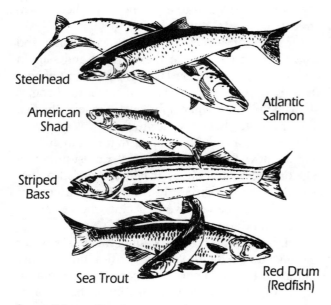

Steelhead

American Shad

Striped Bass

Sea Trout

Atlantic Salmon

Red Drum (Redfish)

Some Estuary Species

For anglers, an estuary offers exciting fishing. Frequently, both freshwater and saltwater species of fish are found in such locations because of the abundance of food.

To find fish in an estuary, anglers seeking a certain species of fish often check the salinity of the water. Looking for other forms of life provides clues. The presence of barnacles, for instance, indicates saltier water; their absence shows less salt in the water.

A number of species (anadromous) spend most of their lives in salt water, but ascend freshwater rivers to spawn, including striped bass, salmon, and shad.

WETLANDS

A wetland is an area of wet, spongy land where the water remains near or above the surface of the ground for most of the year. Wetlands are often found between open water and dry land. There are several types of wetlands, including marshes, swamps and bogs. Wetlands occur in fresh water, salt water, and estuaries. Almost all are teeming with life.

Many people used to think that wetlands were waste areas. For this reason, more than 50 percent of the wetlands in our country have been drained or destroyed. What a mistake!

Wetlands are among the richest lands anywhere in terms of production. A cattail marsh can yield 12 tons of biomass for every acre. Some of this production can be traced to water-level changes. These fluctuations carry and expose nutrients, oxygenate the water, and filter out impurities and sediment. Saltwater wetlands benefit from tides in much the same way. Today we understand that wetlands provide vital spawning habitat for numerous fish, and are also important to birds and mammals. Wetlands also help control floods and store large amounts of water for a long time.

Marshes and swamps are very important areas for fish. Marshes are more open and have grasses, reeds and other non-woody plants. Swamps have many trees and shrubs.

Most **bogs** are found in northern climates. Bogs are areas with acidic soil and a heavy growth of mosses. Peat moss is formed in bogs by the build up and partial decay of plants. Because of the acid water, fish are usually not found in bogs.

SWAMP

BOG

MARSH

RIPARIAN ZONES

Riparian areas are a middle zone of vegetation along streams and rivers. Due to the influence of water, the vegetation in a riparian zone is typically larger and more dense than the vegetation outside the zone.

Riparian Zone

In the drier parts of the country, riparian zones are very obvious. Only the small section near the water has any green vegetation. In parts of the country where more rainfall occurs, riparian zones are not as easy to point out, but they do exist.

Like wetlands, quality riparian areas play a vital role in maintaining the quality of the water in streams and rivers. When humans or livestock destroy the vegetation, the quality of the water is not as good.

Riparian vegetation provides food and shade for aquatic plants and animals. Leaf litter and terrestrial insects fall from vegetation into streams, providing a source of food for fish. Elimination of the vegetation along the river can cause the temperature of the river to rise because there is nothing to shade the water from the sun.

Quality riparian zones act as a sponge in times of heavy rain which assists in the prevention of flooding. When the rains stop and water levels drop in the river, the riparian area slowly releases water back into the river. This helps the river or stream to maintain a more stable water supply for fish and other plants and animals that depend on it. Quality ripar-

ian zones also cleanse water and its vegetation slows water in flood periods, helping it drop some of its sediment load.

THE OCEANS

Oceans cover nearly three-fourths of the earth's surface. The creatures that live in the sea are very different from those that live in fresh water. Almost all ocean plant life is algae, including the giant Pacific kelp and the sargassum weed that coat the surface of tropical seas.

Fish are able to survive from the greatest depths in the ocean to the shallow, intertidal zone. Temperature and water depth, however, limit the distribution of various species.

Features Of The Oceans

The Intertidal Zone. The intertidal zone is a low flat area along the shore. It is the area covered by the sea at high tide and exposed at low tide. Crabs, snails and other creatures live here. Predator fish, like the shark, feed in this shallow area at high tide. Their bellies may scrape the bottom while their fins and backs are out of the water. Many other kinds of fish also feed in this zone because it is rich in food, including mussels, clams, and crabs. On the West Coast, tides can fluctuate 15 to 20 feet. Almost all bank fishing is done in this environment.

The bonefish is a master at following the tide, feasting on crustacea and other animals coming out of their burrows as water floods the area. Snook lie in depressions close to a sandy beach to ambush baitfish. On a shallow flat, anglers can see fish falling back into deeper channels just ahead of the receding water.

Coastal Waters. Coastal waters are seldom as clear as the open ocean. Water temperature affects the variety of creatures in the waters and the warmer coastal water has more forms of life than the colder waters of the open ocean.

In coastal areas, the ocean bottom may have areas of exposed rock, but most is sand or sediment. Fish live at all depths in this inshore water. Most, however, are found close to the bottom. Many feed near some object such as a rock or coral reef, places where they can ambush prey. Other fish roam coastal waters, searching for a meal.

Most saltwater anglers fish in coastal waters because there are dozens of different fish species to choose from. Smart anglers monitor water temperatures to determine which species they should be fishing for. Fish found in this area include bonefish, bluefish, and barracuda.

The Open Ocean. It is worth noting that every part of the sea explored by humans has produced some form of life regardless of depth, water temperature, or amount of light. From a practical standpoint, anglers are only concerned with the top portion of the oceans.

Organisms as tiny as plankton are found in open water. Upwellings bring nutrient-rich waters to the surface where the sun causes more plankton to bloom. Zooplankton feed on the phytoplankton and, in turn, are eaten by baitfish. These baitfish are a source of food for dolphin, tuna, marlin, swordfish, shark, and other open-water species. Flying fish are an open-water species. Dolphin feast on flying fish and marlin attack small dolphin.

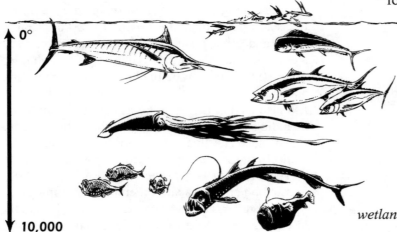

0°

10,000

Saltwater Species

Most kinds of fish that live in deep water grow quickly, at least during their early years. A marlin, for example, grows from the size of a pinhead to 9.5 pounds in 12 weeks!

Recreational angling takes place within the confines of the continental shelf—out to about 200 miles. Several species of game fish cross oceans, but fishing is limited to areas that boats can reach with relative ease and safety. Catching large fish in the open ocean takes special tackle, great skill, stamina, and large, safe boats.

ACTIVITIES

Activity 1—Habitat Scramble

Below are clues which are a partial description of an aquatic community. See if you can identify each type.

*The answers are scrambled.

1. _____ (ssheram) home to grasses, reeds, trees and shrubs
2. _____ (nsiaporirneza—2 words) middle zone of vegetation along streams and rivers
3. _____ (coaaassttlwer—2 words) ocean bottom, has exposed rock, sand or sediment
4. _____ (aeenniittrodlz—2 words) low flat area along ocean shore
5. _____ (anwdetls) ground is wet and spongy, stores water, valuable habitat for wildlife
6. _____ (ssueetari) place where river water mixes with salty ocean water
7. _____ (pndos) tiny lakes and often shaped like a bowl
8. _____ (verrsi) water level and current changes with precipitation

* estuaries, rivers, marshes, intertidal zone, riparian zones, ponds, wetlands, coastal waters

Activity 2—How Muddy is Muddy?

Pour about 1/4 cup water from your fishing area on a white paper plate. Gently lay a piece of absorbent paper toweling over it to soak up the water. When the toweling is wet, remove it. What is left on the plate is the sediment or particles which were suspended in the water.

Another method of assessing the sediment or turbidity of your water sample is to slowly pour the water through the paper toweling. The toweling will act as a filter. Take samples from several aquatic environments in your area. How will the amount of sediment in the water influence your fishing tactics? How could the level of sediment affect aquatic life?

CHAPTER 16

EFFECT OF HUMAN CULTURE ON AQUATIC RESOURCES

Clean, pure water might be our most precious resource. From the beginning of civilization, waterways have been important for food, transportation, and housing. In more recent times water has been used for industrial development, electrical power, and as a necessity in manufacturing. The supply of fresh water and the bounty of the ocean have seemed endless and few people have been concerned with the supply of water, its cleanliness, or the fish populations it contained.

Eventually, farsighted scientists and conservationists argued that growing human development and a disregard for the nation's waterways were destroying valuable fishery resources. They showed the need to develop techniques for managing both water and fishery resources. Fish hatcheries were established in an effort to replace declining fish populations. Early efforts, however, often failed because fishery managers and others did not fully understand that fish habitat had to be improved before fish stocking would be effective for real, long-term results.

Today, fisheries management is much more of an exact science than it was in its early days. Now, dedicated people try to improve the habitat that is left.

FACTORS IN AQUATIC RESOURCE MANAGEMENT

Waterways Allocations

Water is necessary for farming, manufacturing, commerce, housing developments, hydroelectric power and many recreational pursuits. Although the need for water may be vital, some uses can harm bodies of water. For example, the large amount of water needed to produce aluminum might affect water usage in an area. If not monitored and treated, water used and released in chemical and steel production will pollute waterways. Damming a stream for flood control or irrigation may restrict water flow downstream. Some streams have "minimum stream flows" established by law to reserve enough water to keep populations alive. A reservoir formed for recreation might be applauded by swimmers, water skiers, boaters, and lake anglers, but ruin the recreation of river canoeists, stream anglers, and white water rafters. Because of conflicting needs for water, some balance must be reached to assure that everyone is treated fairly.

Watersheds

The aquatic habitat is often negatively impacted by activities that take place far from the water body. We all understand that water runs downhill. The **land area** from which the water drains to a common outlet such as a stream or river is a watershed.

Watersheds are mostly land areas and every bit of land on earth is in a watershed. Yards and streets are elements of a watershed from which water runs off to feed a nearby stream. Small and medium-sized watersheds make up larger ones. The Mississippi River drains

Watershed

a watershed of more than one million square miles and is made up of thousands of smaller watersheds. What happens in one small watershed also affects the larger watershed it is a part of.

If water does not evaporate or soak into the soil, it usually drains into a waterway. However, if the water runs off the land too fast, the water carries off topsoil and cuts gullies. The soil, along with other debris and pollutants that flow off watersheds into streams and lakes, may spoil fishing. When too much water flows off the watershed, it causes floods. Therefore, the management of the land surrounding bodies of water has a great bearing on water quality, and the fish that live in the watershed.

Habitat Degradation

No part of the United States is completely immune from the degradation of habitat. Poor logging practices allow rain waters to carry silt and soil that reduce the clarity of rivers and streams, harming habitat and fish populations. Trees and other debris left from harvesting timber often alter the natural flow of rivers and streams.

Wetlands are often drained to make logging and farming easier. In the Mississippi River plain only one-fifth of the original 24 million acres of wetland habitat remains.

In the name of flood control, many meandering waterways have been channelized, or straightened, destroying precious habitat and fishery resources. The Florida Everglades is one such victim of artificially controlled water flows. Both freshwater and saltwater species of fish have been negatively affected by this attempt to prevent flooding.

During part of their lives, about two-thirds of saltwater species rely on estuaries for survival. Even those species which remain in

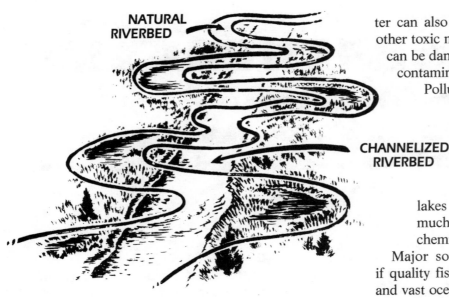

NATURAL RIVERBED

CHANNELIZED RIVERBED

deep water often feed on fish that need an estuary to live. Precious estuary habitat diminishes at an alarming rate still today. Pollution is one reason for this decline, but dredging, filling, bulkheading, and other construction creates serious problems.

TYPES OF POLLUTION

All kinds of things end up in our waters, lowering their quality. Some pollution, like land erosion, occurs naturally. Most, however, is caused by humans.

Those concerned about pollution refer to two kinds of pollution, **point-source** and **non-point-source.**

Point-source pollution can be traced to a definite point where it enters the environment. Point-source pollution can come from industries that dump wastes, chemicals, or heavy metals. Toxic waste dumps, mining operations, accidental chemical or oil spills and waste-water treatment plants are also point-source pollution sites.

Non-point-source pollution is more difficult to identify because it doesn't enter water at an easy-to-locate place. Often it is caused by herbicides, pesticides, and fertilizers used on orchards, farms, and lawns which eventually enter waterways. Animal wastes are another common source.

Metals are often present in waste materials from industrial plants. Fish have trouble living in water containing small amounts of copper and zinc. Ammonia, chlorine, and fluorine in water can also kill fish. Mercury, dioxin, PCBs and other toxic materials not only can kill fish, but also can be dangerous to humans and wildlife that eat contaminated fish.

Pollution problems may differ depending upon where you live. In the Northeastern U.S., acid rain is a big problem to fish and other wildlife. Along Lake Superior asbestos particles from mining waste has been a problem. Mercury is a concern in many lakes in Minnesota and Wisconsin. Around much of the Great Lakes, PCBs and other chemicals cause distress.

Major sources of pollution must be stopped if quality fisheries are to exist. Even the estuaries and vast oceans of the world are fragile ecosystems that require attention and careful use in order to be protected.

Acid Rain

Acid rain is one of the biggest problems facing the quality of our water today, and many bodies of water are suffering from its effects. Acid rain is a result of industries and autos burning oil and coal (fossil fuels) for fuel. Industry smokestacks and automobile tailpipes send sulfur dioxide and nitrogen oxides high into the atmosphere. These elements can remain in the air for several days and travel hundreds of miles. While in the air they mix with water vapor and turn into sulfuric and nitric acids. This harmful acid returns to earth in rain, hail, fog, dew, sleet, snow, or as dry particles. This acid damages plant life and may eventually kill insects, frogs, and fish in our waters.

Acid Rain

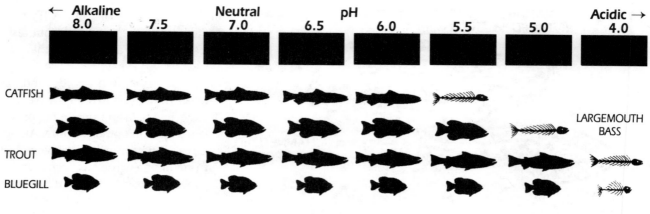

pH Scale

The amount of acid in liquids is measured on a scale from 0 to 14. This is called the **pH** scale. A pH of 7.0 (distilled water) is in the middle of the scale and is considered neutral—neither acidic nor alkaline. Things below 7.0 such as lemon juice (pH of 2.0) are acidic. Things above 7.0, like ammonia (pH 11.0), are alkaline.

The pH scale is logarithmic. This means that a pH of 6 is *10* times more acidic than a pH of 7. A pH of 5 is *100* times more acidic than a pH of 7 and a pH of 4 is *1,000* times more acidic than a pH of 7.

Because carbon dioxide and water found naturally in the atmosphere have a pH of 5.0 to 5.6, natural rain is slightly acidic. However, acid rain that falls in the Northeastern United States often ranges from 4.0 to 4.6 pH. In most regions of the country the lakes and rivers can tolerate this acidity without any loss of water quality. A natural buffering ability present in most soils that contain limestone can neutralize acidity. However, several regions of the country are damaged by acid rain because they have thin soils and granite bedrock. Granite is low in limestone and cannot neutralize (buffer) acid precipitation.

The Northeast, the Rocky Mountains, areas of the Northcentral and Southeastern U.S., and Eastern Canada are most affected by acid rain.

Once a body of water contains too much acid, the creatures in the water's food chain begin to die. Eggs and larvae are sensitive to low pH and unable to survive. As water becomes more acid, the fertility of eggs is reduced, fewer hatch, and fish may not grow to adult sizes. Eventually insects, the fishes' food, or even the fish, may no longer be able to live in water with a low pH.

Acid rain is a worldwide problem because it can be carried great distances in the atmosphere before falling back to earth. Pollution sources in midwestern states can actually harm waters on the east coast! As a result, thousands of lakes in the United States, Canada, and other countries are suffering from its effects. If steps are not taken to reduce acid rain, many more bodies of water may be ruined.

How You Can Help Reduce Acid Rain:

- Car pool whenever possible.
- Make sure gasoline powered vehicles have their engines properly tuned.
- Conserve electrical use in the home. Oil and phosphate fuels and high sulfur coal are used at many power plants and contribute to acid rain.

Silt or Sediment

Silt and sediment are fine particles of soil or sand in our waters. A small amount of sediment reaching the water is natural. However, poor surface mining, logging, construction, and farming practices can leave soil unstable. Poorly regulated grazing in and near streams can also be a problem. Then, when it rains, the soil is carried off by the water and eventually runs into a river or lake. Fortunately, there are modern methods of farming, logging and mining that reduce erosion.

When silt or sediment settles, it has a smothering effect. It can kill plants or other small organisms; it can smother fish eggs and young aquatic life; it can cover up the rocks where the fish's food lives. If the silt does not settle, the water ends up with a dirty look. This muddy water does not allow light for use by plants and other aquatic life. The result is a ruined body of water that no longer supports the fish we want to catch.

Agricultural Wastes

Agricultural wastes include manure, liquid and granular fertilizers, silo liquids, and pesticides. Cattle, hogs, sheep, and poultry raised on feed lots are a big problem to aquatic organisms because they concentrate a lot of waste over a very small area. One cow produces as much waste as 17 people every day. Some of this waste is washed directly into streams and rivers. In addition, farmers spread manure and fertilizer that may eventually enter a body of water.

Pesticides are chemicals used to help farmers control pests that ruin their crops. If properly used, they generally create little or no problem. However, when they enter a water system through careless use, they usually cause environmental damage by killing fish and other organisms in the water.

Sewage

Sewage consists of human waste and garbage that deplete the dissolved oxygen in water. Sewage wastes contain nutrients that serve as fertilizers. They cause algae (tiny plants) to bloom in great quantities. When these organisms die, oxygen is used for the process of decomposition, and the fish go without adequate oxygen and sometimes die. If this situation gets bad enough, all the fish in a river below a treatment plant may die.

Raw sewage can also cause serious diseases in humans who use the water or eat shellfish from polluted areas. Sewage may also make waters unhealthy to swim in.

What You Can Do:

- Don't make sewage treatment more difficult by dumping chemical or other cleansing agents in drains or in the toilet.
- If your house is on a septic system instead of a city sewer system, it is important to service the system periodically.

Industrial Waste

Most industries produce some form of liquid waste that has to be treated before it is released into public waters. These waste waters may contain many toxic chemicals. Although some discharges are treated, some of this chemical waste is still discharged directly into aquatic systems.

What You Can Do To Reduce Industrial Waste:

- Recycle. Some industrial waste can be reduced by recycling.

- Write your legislator. Express the importance of having strong legislation to protect our water resources.
- Never pour anything into a storm drain. Household chemicals, paints, or soaps dumped down the gutter flow into streams untreated.

Petroleum Products

Accidental oil spills can have disastrous effects on aquatic life. Petroleum products can kill by direct contact with the fish's gills. Oil can also suffocate eggs and young fish because the young inhabit shallow waters where oil tends to concentrate. Marine birds, sea otters and turtles may also be killed.

What You Can Do To Reduce Petroleum Wastes:

- Recycle used automotive oil. Drain the oil from your vehicle into a container and take it to a service station that recycles oil. Do not pour it down a storm drain!

Trash

We have become a throw-away society and are running out of places to put our trash. Some people do not even try to dispose of their trash appropriately and throw it along our waters. No one enjoys fishing or swimming while having to contend with broken bottles, sharp cans, and other trash. Sinking cans, bottles or other trash in the water may put them out of sight temporarily, but they are still there and can cause long-term problems.

Plastics are particularly hazardous. They are not easily biodegradable and will be around for a long time, perhaps for hundreds of years. Thousands of fish and birds die every year from entanglement in plastic six-pack rings that come from canned drinks. Nylon fishing line, discarded by thoughtless anglers, can also entangle and kill birds. Some sea turtles even mistake plastic bags for jellyfish (their favorite food) and choke to death when they eat a bag by mistake.

What You Can Do To Reduce Trash:

- Recycle! Always dispose of your trash properly, especially plastics. If you see trash around your favorite fishing spot, pick it up for recycling or place it in a garbage can where it belongs. Carry a litter bag at all times.
- If you see your friends littering, explain to them that they may be doing a lot more harm than they realize. Don't let them sink cans, bottles or other trash in a lake or stream.
- Before discarding, cut up large tangles of fishing line into short sections. Some places collect fishing line for recycling. Also, cut up six-pack plastic rings. This little extra effort will help save fish, birds and other aquatic animals and will probably make you feel good too.

Exotic Introductions and Nuisance Species

Exotic species become **nuisance species** when they adversely upset the delicate balance of a particular body of water where they are introduced. These may be considered biological pollutants.

Fishery managers are aware of the effects of introducing new fish species into bodies of water. Before introducing new species, the ecosystem must be studied carefully.

In the Great Lakes, coho and chinook salmon from the Pacific Ocean are positive, intentional introductions of exotic species. Exotic species can compete with native fish for food, space, and spawning habitat. Some exotics, however, have filled a vacant niche in various ecosystems. The brown trout, striped bass, and Pacific salmon are positive examples of this. However, accidental introductions can cause serious problems. These include sea lamprey that prey on salmon and trout and zebra mussel that clog water intake pipes in many areas.

In some bodies of water a particular type of fish or vegetation may be part of the balance. However, in a different body of water the same fish or plant may throw off the entire balance.

Crappie are excellent sport fish and they fit in well in many lake ecosystems. However, if put into a different setting, crappie can ruin the balance of an entire lake. In the wrong setting, crappie populate faster and compete for food and space with other fish, upsetting this balance. This could result in a lot of small crappie and little else.

Certain kinds of vegetation might be healthy for some water systems. In others, that same plant/weed might take over. Too much vegetation can interfere with boating access and protect small fish, creating an overpopulation. Also, when weeds die, they decompose, thus removing oxygen from the water. When the oxygen level gets too low, fish will die.

What You Can Do To Prevent Nuisance Species:

- Never release fish from one body of water into another.
- Never release fish or vegetation from an aquarium.
- Never dump left-over live bait into a lake or river.
- Remove aquatic weeds from trailers and boats and discard them before moving to another lake.

INDIVIDUAL IMPACT

Major sources of pollution must be stopped if quality fisheries are to exist. Even the large oceans and estuaries of the world are fragile ecosystems that require attention and careful use to protect them for future use and enjoyment.

We can all help. While many of these problems seem out of your hands, there are many problems you can solve in your area by getting your classmates, friends, and neighbors to vocally protest the problem.

Our own daily actions are important. We each have a responsibility to make sure our own actions are not depleting or polluting the water. An individual action, either positive or negative, may seem small. However, when you multiply that by millions of us who live in each state, these actions can have a tremendous cumulative impact.

Responsible anglers are knowledgeable about different types of pollution and other factors that degrade fishery resources. They use this knowledge to express their views to state legislators and congressional representatives.

ACTIVITIES

Activity 1—The Effect Of Acid Rain

We hear a great deal about acid rain and its effect on the environment. Acid rain can turn some bodies of water to a solution similar to vinegar. Here is a simple demonstration to show one impact of acid rain: Put a chicken leg bone in a jar and add enough vinegar to cover it. Examine it 2–3 days later. Next, leave it for 2–3 more days and examine once again. The vinegar has weakened the bone structure.

Crayfish use minerals in the water to produce their shells or exoskeletons. Some of these minerals are in the bone. Since vinegar is an acid, what conclusions can you draw from your observations?

Activity 2—Oil and Eggs Don't Mix?

Chicken eggs are similar to fish eggs. Both have a porous covering which allow gases to enter and leave the egg. This transfer is essential for development of the embryo. Place a fresh chicken's egg in a two-cup liquid measure almost full of water. Notice the bubbles forming on the egg's surface. Let it sit for 5 minutes and check again. Gently tap the side of the cup. What happens to the bubbles? Now take your egg out and dry it completely. Cover it with vegetable oil or lard. Place it back in the water. What difference in bubble formation do you see? What might happen to fish eggs in an oil spill?

Activity 3—Plastic in the Environment

Plastics are both friend and foe. They serve many useful purposes. However, when they become trash carelessly thrown out in the environment or become a major component of a land fill, they spell trouble.

Collect the trash from a sizable area around your favorite fishing spot. How much of it is plastic? Plastics require hundreds of years to break down, or biodegrade. To observe this, bury several of the plastic items you collected in one corner of your garden or yard. Along with the plastic, you might want to include some vegetable peelings or material you have left from preparing your fish for cooking. Cover your items and let them stay there undisturbed for six months to a year. Then dig them up and examine each item. Can you determine which items left in or around a pond will decay? Which will be left to litter the environment and perhaps cause harm to wildlife?

Activity 4—What is your Watershed Address?

Where does water go that flows off the streets and yards around your house or apartment? If it flows into a drain, ask your public works department to tell you where the drainage from your property eventually ends up. What streams, rivers, or wetlands might the drainage impact if harmful items like oil, plastic and other trash, soil, and chemicals enter the drain?

CHAPTER 17

MANAGING FISH FOR EVERYONE

Today, around 60 million Americans fish. Because of this large demand for fishing, management of fishery resources is extremely important and involves people management as well.

One of the problems fishery managers face is that good fishing to one person, may not be good fishing to another. Some anglers don't care what they catch as long as they catch something. Other anglers are only interested in a certain species of fish. Some want to catch lots of fish, while others want big fish. Still others don't care if they catch anything as long as they get to relax in the beautiful outdoors.

CONSERVATION

Conservation involves the wise use of habitat and other resources with the thought of preserving and protecting these resources for the use of future generations. It is based on an understanding of basic biological principles and requires knowing about the levels of production that can be sustained from an ecosystem and the effects of harvesting on the population of a given species. Conservation also demands an awareness of environmental factors that may help or harm a fishery.

Poaching, overharvesting, and destructive land and water practices are all areas of concern that are damaging to conservation efforts. These are best addressed through education to create increased understanding and broad support of basic conservation principles along with vigorous law enforcement.

CONSERVATION VS. PRESERVATION

Minerals and oil are examples of nonrenewable resources. When they are removed from the ground, there is no way to produce more. Other resources such as fish and other animals, forests and other plant life, are renewable.

Fish not caught and used will die and be replaced by others of the same species. Most conservationists believe that the wise use of renewable resources, including the harvesting of timber, hunting animals, and fishing, can be enjoyed without destroying the resource. Conservation, however, does require careful monitoring of these resources so that their base is not harmed.

Preservationists believe that taking of natural resources is wrong and that fish, game, and forests should not be used in any way. Most professional managers regard this view as unrealistic.

Fish Stocking

FISHERY MANAGEMENT

Managing Fish Populations

A fishery manager must first consider the habitat in order to manage fish. As you have learned, fish require the right water temperature, oxygen level, food sources and cover. Stocking trout in warm water is a waste since they would not survive very long. Likewise, if pike are placed in a lake without vegetation, they wouldn't do well either.

Most fish spawn naturally and produce their own young. In these cases, a fishery manager does not have to stock fish every year. The fish replenish the waters on their own. A biologist will then manage the fishery by improving the habitat, regulating the catch and trying to balance the populations of fish species sharing the aquatic environment.

Hatcheries and Fish Stocking

Even though fish stocking is costly and isn't always necessary or possible, in the right situation, it can be a valuable tool to enhance sport fishing. Federal and state hatcheries raise many kinds of fish for stocking. Most raise freshwater fish, but saltwater species such as striped bass, red drum, snook, and sea trout are now being raised successfully.

Fry, the smallest size of fish stocked, are the least costly, but many die after release. Adult fish survive better but cost more to raise. Many states stock a combination of large and small fish each year. States often stock trout because they are easy to raise, are good sport fish, and are less expensive than other species.

Why stock trout in a lake if the yellow perch fishing is great? Why risk upsetting the balance in a great bass lake by stocking northern pike? Fisheries managers realize that each lake or river has its own unique combination of fish. This assortment of fish represents the "carrying capacity" of that aquatic system. Smart anglers know that if they sample different waters, they will discover a wide variety of fish. They also know that all of them are fun to catch and just about all of them are great to eat.

Habitat Improvement

An important key in fishery management is habitat protection and improvement.

Aquatic vegetation is important for fish in most waters. It supplies oxygen, attracts food, and offers protection. However, too many weeds are harmful and can "choke a lake." To manage weed growth, cutting, poisoning, uprooting, and introducing fish that eat weeds have all been tried. One of the best controls is limiting the plant food that enters the water in the form of sewage, fertilizers, or farm waste.

The habitat in streams and rivers can be improved by building small dams to raise the water level in pools, strengthening banks with rock, logs, and vegetation, and creating hiding places for fish with logs or brush.

Building artificial reefs to attract and provide a refuge for both freshwater and saltwater species is another way to improve some fisheries. Artificial reefs can be as simple as sinking weighted Christmas trees in a lake or as complex as sinking an old ship offshore in the ocean. Reefs are important because they provide an area for the bottom of the food chain to develop. This is a source of food and cover for baitfish and game fish. Always check with management authorities before attempting to put something in the water to attract fish. You may need a permit to place structures in a lake or stream. If you haven't guessed by now, reefs are good places to fish.

State agencies work to improve habitat, but fishing clubs, scout troops, businesses, and local community groups supervised by state or federal fisheries staff can provide valuable assistance on local projects.

Habitat Improvement

Working to improve water quality by reducing the amount of pollution entering the water is one of the best methods of improving fish habitat. It is important for citizens to voice their opinion to city officials, state legislators, and congressional representatives on the importance of protecting the water quality.

Fishing Pressure

People management is also an important consideration in fisheries management. Biologists must consider the increasing fishing pressure caused not only because more people are taking up angling, but also because the average angler is more knowledgeable and has more technological advances available to him.

Underutilized Species

Heavier fishing pressure would benefit some fish populations, including sunfish, perch, and bullheads, and could relieve the amount of stocking required for more sought-after species. Many anglers don't even know these fish are there just waiting to be caught! Without enough angling pressure, panfish may overpopulate a lake or pond, resulting in many very small fish. This phenomenon, called "stunting" can be helped by anglers who take some of these panfish home for dinner. More and more anglers are also discovering that these panfish can be the most delicious fish to eat and are also fun to catch!

Fishing Regulations

Fishing regulations protect the resource and help all anglers enjoy more success. The fact that most anglers must have a fishing license is an example of a fishing regulation. In most states, those who are under or over certain ages do not need a license.

Other regulations may:

- **Set a limit on how many fish of a certain species you can take in one day.**
- **Set a starting and an ending date for a fishing season.**
- **Set a limit on the number of fishing lines and hooks that you are allowed to use.**

- **Set size limits for fish.**
- **Set a slot limit so that anglers can only keep fish over and under a certain size.**

Some states have fishing laws that apply throughout the state. Other states may have different regulations for different bodies of water. No matter where you fish, know what the regulations are for the area you are fishing.

There are good reasons for fishing laws. All are intended to conserve and improve fish populations. Fisheries biologists often study bodies of water and suggest a new law if it will help keep the fish population healthy. For example, if there is a fishing season in your state, it may have been introduced to protect fish during spawning or as a way of limiting the number of fish caught on heavily fished waters. Size limits are also meant to protect fish of spawning size before they are caught.

Fishing laws are also intended to make it possible for more people to share in a fishery. Daily fish limits are meant to keep people from taking too many fish at one time. Those who do take more fish than the law allows are considered poachers, whom conservation officers work to arrest. You can help conservation officers protect your fish, forests, and wildlife by obeying the laws and reporting any violations that you see. Some states have a special telephone number for reporting fish and game violations.

Fisheries Research

To do their job, fishery biologists need as much information about a fishery as possible. They try to learn the needs of anglers and the condition of fish populations.

Biologists also need to know how many fish are being caught. They sometimes do this by taking information from anglers after a day of fishing. Sometimes biologists study fish by collecting them. Biologists also mark fish with special tags or clip one or more of their fins. When marked fish are collected later, the biologists can learn many things. A tag or fin clip can tell them how fast fish are growing, how many are caught, and how far they have traveled.

After studying this information, biologists try to decide the best ways to produce more and better fishing for anglers while still conserving the resource.

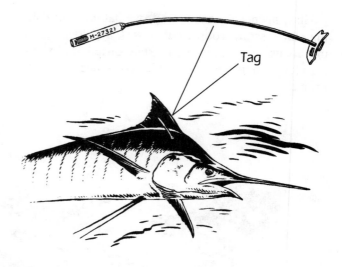

Tag

Tagged Fish

Financing Our Aquatic Resources

Do you know who pays for most of the research and other efforts to improve sport fisheries? Anglers do—the same people who use and enjoy them! Some money comes from the sale of fishing licenses and special-use stamps. Other money comes from a special government program, called the Federal Aid in Sport Fish Restoration Program. Some people also refer to this program as "Dingell-Johnson" or "Wallop-Breaux." Here's how this government program works:

When an angler buys fishing tackle and a boater buys fuel, they each pay a tax that goes into a fund. Other money comes from a tax on the sale of tackle and boats imported from other countries. All of this money is then shared by the states to help pay for certain projects. The project may be building a public fishing pond or a large fish hatchery. The money can also be used to pay for managing fisheries, fisheries research, or for teaching people about the environment, conservation, water safety, and fishing. Each year, the Federal Aid in Sport Fish Restoration Program provides more than $200 million for such purposes.

Your purchase of fishing equipment and motorboat fuels supports Sport Fishing Restoration and boating access facilities

YOUR ROLE

Knowing the purpose of fishing regulations, the consequences of dumping pollutants or toxic wastes, the result of clear-cutting crops or forests all the way to a shoreline, or otherwise destroying habitat, is important to the preservation of our resources. Education is necessary if conservation is to be a meaningful, workable, and understandable concept rather than an abstract theory with no practical application. A lack of conservation practices by only a few can affect the beauty of the outdoors, the pleasure received from all water-related sports, and the quality of the angling experience.

You can help those whose job it is to protect and improve our waters and fish populations. One way is to know and to obey the laws for the waters you fish. You can also do the following:

- **Practice catch-and-release if you don't plan to eat a fish.**

- **If you catch a tagged or fin-clipped fish, report it to your state's natural resources agency.**
- **After fishing, leave the fishing spot cleaner than you found it. Never litter and do your best to remove any trash left by others.**
- **Get involved and support good conservation laws and programs.**
- **Teach others about our valuable aquatic resources and how to help conserve them.**
- **Report poachers to your local conservation officer.**

Through your efforts, we will all have good places to fish for years to come!

ACTIVITIES

Activity 1—Helping With Litter

Every angler should make it a point to improve the environment. One of the easiest and most productive ways of doing this is to recycle. Set up a recycling area in your home. Set aside containers for plastics, aluminum, paper, glass and other recyclables. Go one step further and bring home a dozen beverage cans from your fishing area every time you go out. Pick up those hunks of old fishing line you see lying on the ground. If we all do this, just think what a difference it will make.

Activity 2—Conservation Practices

Individuals concerned about the future of fishing need to take an active part in organizations that are striving to protect habitat for wildlife. These include many state organizations and others that operate nationwide. Examples of national organizations are the American Sportfishing Association, the Bass Anglers Sportsmens Society, the Izaak Walton League, the National Wildlife Federation, and Trout Unlimited. Get involved in an organization of your own choosing.

Activity 3—A Lot of Water Down The Drain

Below are the projected populations for the United States for the years 1995 and 2000. If each of these persons will use 70 gallons daily, how much water will be used daily in the United States in each of these years? What is the total amount that might be used for one week in the year 1995? 2000? Assume a population of 249,657,000 in 1995 and 267,955,000 in 2000.

123

FISHING FOR A CAREER!

Many people would love to have a job that's related to fishing, and there are many career opportunities for people interested in aquatic resources and the out-of-doors. Whether you're interested in teaching, biology, ecology, business, research, law enforcement, sales, writing, conservation, or various aspects of fishing, there is an option for you.

Federal, state and private agencies employ people with interests and skills in many of these job categories. Thirty-seven different federal agencies have some responsibility for managing fish populations on their lands. Examples include the U.S. Forest Service, National Park Service, Bureau of Land Management, and the U.S. Army Corps of Engineers. Two federal agencies have federal authority for en-

forcing federal laws regarding the fishery. Basically, the U.S. Fish and Wildlife Service is in charge of freshwater and the National Marine Fisheries Service is in charge of saltwater.

THE U.S. FISH AND WILDLIFE SERVICE

The U.S. Fish and Wildlife Service is a federal government agency in the Department of the Interior. The Service manages a system of national wildlife refuges for migratory birds and a system of fish hatcheries and research areas in an effort to improve wildlife and fish resources.

The Fish and Wildlife Service is also responsible for enforcing several federal laws. These include the Endangered Species Act, the Marine Mammal Protection Act, and the Migratory Bird Treaty Act.

The Fish and Wildlife Service also administers federal money to state governments, gives technical help to state and foreign governments, takes part in international meetings on wildlife conservation, and keeps the public informed about the condition of America's fish and wildlife resources.

THE NATIONAL MARINE FISHERIES SERVICE

The National Marine Fisheries Service is a federal government agency in the Department of Commerce. It provides management, research, and service for the protection of saltwater (marine) species. It also enforces the federal laws governing saltwater fish and mammals. This includes regulating both the taking of sport fish and commercially harvested living marine resources.

STATE NATURAL RESOURCES AGENCIES

The name of the state agency that deals with fisheries and wildlife varies from state to state. Some examples are: Department of Natural Resources; Department of Conservation; Department of Fish and Game; Game and Fish Commission; Department of Fisheries, Wildlife, and Environmental Law; and Department of Environmental Protection. You should find out what it is called in your state.

State Natural Resources Agencies protect and improve our waters and fisheries by:

1. **Raising and stocking fish**
2. **Improving habitat for fish**
3. **Developing regulations to protect the resource**
4. **Conducting research on fish populations**
5. **Teaching citizens how to fish and to conserve resources**
6. **Using the media to keep the public informed**

Fisheries Biologists

Each state, and many federal agencies employ many fisheries biologists who help manage fish populations. Fisheries biologists must have an interest in the science of biology. In high school it's helpful to study life sciences. In college, a student should study aquatic biology and other related science courses. Today, math, statistics, computer science, public speaking and writing are other areas biologists need to complete their science degree.

Fisheries biologists often work outdoors where they gather information and samples for study. Such information helps them to manage and conserve fish populations and protect the environment. They must have a good knowledge of fish and how they live. They also must know the interests of anglers and others who use the state's resources. When indoors, writing and computer skills aid them in completing reports.

Law Enforcement Officers

State natural resources agencies also enforce state laws designed to protect natural resources. The people who do this were once called "fish and game wardens," but now some are called "conservation police," "wildlife officers," or "law enforcement officers." Today, however, such officers do more than enforce laws that protect fish, forests, and wildlife. They also enforce environmental and pollution laws, and play an active role in fish and wildlife management. In some states they have the same authority as a state police officer.

Fish Hatchery Manager

People who raise fish in hatcheries or fish farms practice a skill called aquaculture. State hatcheries raise fish for stocking. Private fish farms may raise fish for bait, food or stocking. Hatcheries raise everything from trout, bass, and catfish to striped bass and drum in both fresh and saltwater.

TEACHERS

Teachers who teach biology, ecology, and other sciences, including the study of fisheries, are needed at all educational levels including elementary, junior high and high school, as well as in colleges and universities. They may teach in the classroom or in the outdoors and some may do research. Teachers need patience and a desire to work with young people.

CONSERVATION REPRESENTATIVES

Many non-profit groups are interested and involved in the outdoors, including efforts related to fisheries. The Izaak Walton League of America, Trout Unlimited, the American Sportfishing Association, and the National Wildlife Federation, among others, are interested in our aquatic resources. These organizations have representatives who study laws and regulations, work to pass federal and state laws, represent anglers before the U.S. Congress and state governments, plan volunteer work, and publish newsletters and other materials to keep the public informed.

BUSINESS OPPORTUNITIES

If you think that you would like to go into business for yourself, you have several options.

Tackle Shop Dealers

Tackle shop owners are in a field related to fishing, but their busiest times are when others are fishing. Tackle shop work involves long hours. Those selling live bait may open at 4 a.m. and close as late as 9 p.m. each day. A few may even be open 24 hours a day at certain times of the season. To be successful you must have a good business background and experience, knowledge of fishing and tackle, and an interest in serving the public.

Fishing Guides

You may know a fishing guide in your hometown. Guides provide boats, tackle, and fishing experience to paying customers. A successful guide must have the ability to locate fish, be able to get along with people, and have a desire to take anglers to fishing areas and help them catch fish. Most guides work part-time and may have another job. For example, a teacher may guide on weekends or in the summer. Many tournament anglers began their careers as fishing guides.

Charter Boat Captains

Charter captains are much like fishing guides. They usually operate larger boats that hold six (charter boat license) or more (party boat license), paying customers. Charter boat captains must be licensed. Most operate their business along the seacoasts or on the Great Lakes. Charter boats range from about 20 to 55 feet in length. Some captains own their own boat; others operate them for their owners. Most charter captains have another job because they can't charter all year long. Some may move to another location to continue chartering year-round. For example, some Great Lakes charter captains travel south for the winter to work in warmer climates.

Commercial Fishermen

Commercial fishermen harvest fish to sell for food. They work with nets, traps, and long lines. The hours can be long and the work difficult and dangerous, especially in severe weather. When the fishing is good, the pay can be high. The work, however, is affected by many things, including government regulations, foreign imports, levels of fish stocks, pollution, breakdown of equipment, and economic conditions.

Fishing Tackle Manufacturer

Many people have begun tackle businesses with little money. They have started producing products in the home or garage for local sales, with some eventually building plants to produce and sell their products across the country. Today, some people start a small tackle business and succeed with good or unusual products. However, there is considerable competition in the tackle industry and some find it difficult to make a profit.

Much fishing tackle is currently made in other countries and imported into the U.S. because it is cheaper to do so. So some of the best jobs in the tackle industry are in areas related to the sale and marketing of tackle.

Manufacturer's Sales Representative

Tackle manufacturers depend on local or regional sales firms to sell their products to distributors and dealers. Sales representatives, often called "reps," own their own sales and marketing companies and contract with manufacturers to distribute tackle and equipment.

A sales rep is often responsible for selling in a number of states and must do a considerable amount of traveling. A rep must enjoy meeting people, have good selling ability, know fishing and fishing tackle, and have a good business education and experience in sales, promotion, or marketing.

PRINT AND BROADCAST MEDIA

Numerous career opportunities are open to you if you have an interest in journalism or radio or TV.

Outdoor Writers

Outdoor writers write about different kinds of recreational activities. Subjects include freshwater and saltwater fishing, hunting, camping, boating, hiking, canoeing, bird watching, photography, skiing, and many other outdoor pastimes.

Many colleges have schools or offer courses in journalism. Most writers in this field have a love of the outdoors and begin by writing and selling articles and columns to state or regional magazines and smaller newspapers. Some become full-time outdoors communicators with a large newspaper or national magazine. Others remain "free-lance" writers where they sell their written articles to a variety of newspapers or outdoor magazines or write books for publication. A college degree in journalism or English is very helpful for this career field.

Publishers

Publishers produce magazines, newspapers, newsletters, fishing annuals, regional and local guidebooks, and other publications. They are often in charge of the entire publication, including editorial and advertising workers. They also arrange the printing, distribution, and sales of the publications. A publisher must have knowledge of business, editing, advertising, printing costs, and many other things.

Broadcast Media

Many radio and television stations offer outdoors programs on fishing and other topics. These programs have become very popular with a large audience. Some tournament and other well-known anglers have become the stars of these programs. In addition, the production of radio and television programs requires the talents of producers and directors, skilled technical people, cameramen, writers, and other specialists. Many colleges and universities offer degrees in radio and television, often in the area of journalism.

TOURNAMENT ANGLERS

A growing number of professional anglers fish tournaments for money. Very few of them, however, can make a sufficient full-time living from tournament winnings. Many receive endorsements from tackle manufacturers, conduct seminars at sport shows, and develop television or radio programs or video tapes on fishing. Even with these opportunities, many professional anglers have other full-time jobs. Tournament angling is very competitive, demands a lot of angling skill, stamina, traveling, and sometimes luck to be successful.

OTHER CAREERS

There are many other careers that are related to fishing in some way. They include aquatic scientists for business, industry, and consulting firms; tour guides for local, state, and national parks and recreation areas; recreation specialists; research biologists; and environmental educators. College degrees are required for many of these jobs, but many exciting and challenging careers are waiting for you.

GLOSSARY

Acid Rain—Comes from sulphur compounds in the air which originate from coal burning factories and auto emissions.

Action—Describes how a rod bends. Rods with bend in the tip are called fast action; rods that bend evenly throughout their length are called parabolic.

Adaptation—The ability of a species to accommodate to its environment to satisfy its basic needs of food, comfort (security), and reproduction.

Adipose—Relating to animal fat. The fatty fin on some fish such as catfish and bullheads.

Aerator—An electric air pump used to maintain oxygen levels in live wells or bait containers.

Algae—Simple, photosynthetic plants with one celled organs of reproduction.

Anadromous—Any species of fish that lives in salt water and spawns in fresh water. Species include salmon, shad, perch, striped bass.

Anal—Located near the anus. The fin found on the lower portion of a fish's body near the tail.

Antireverse Lever—A lever or knob that prevents the reel handles from turning backwards as a fish tries to take line.

Backing—A soft, strong fishing line, such as braided dacron that is wound onto a fly reel before the fly line is added.

Backlash—Line tangled on a casting reel as a result of a cast when the spool continues to revolve after the line has stopped going off the reel.

Bail—A wire half-round device that spools the line onto an open-face spinning reel.

Bail Roller—A small roller bearing-like device on one end of the bail over which line rolls when it is retrieved.

Bail Spring—A small spring used to operate a bail on a spinning reel.

Baitcasting—Casting equipment that uses a bait-casting reel, also called a "level-wind."

Barb—The spur found on the point of most fish hooks to lessen the chance of a fish escaping.

Barbel—A whisker-like projection from the jaws of some fish, such as carp or catfish. They help fish smell and feel.

Bass Boat—A boat designed and built for bass fishing.

Bass Bug—A floating, hard bodied bug, usually made of cork or plastic and tied with feathers which is designed to catch bass or panfish.

Blank—The basic shaft of fiberglass, graphite or other type of fishing rod. All are tapered, have a different power and action, and are designed for a specific style of fishing.

Bobber—Used to float on the surface and to suspend a rigging of terminal tackle, usually consisting of a baited hook and sinker. Sometimes call a cork.

Bow—The forward part of a boat.

Bridge Gaff—A gaff that is like a grappling hook attached to a line, used from a bridge or pier to land fish.

Buzzbait—A bass fishing lure designed to run on the surface, creating a disturbance with a large blade.

Cane Pole—Equipment that uses a long, slender rod and no reel. Cane poles are sometimes called "bank poles."

Carnivore—A flesh-eating animal.

Catadromous—A species of fish that lives in fresh water and spawns in salt water, such as eels.

Catfish—A group of scaleless fish named for the long barbels around their mouth that resemble "cat whiskers."

Caudal—Related to or being a tail; the tail fin.

Chart—A "map" of water areas. Charts pinpoint shoals, wrecks, rocks, shorelines, shallows, and other danger areas.

Charter Boat—A boat that is available for charter and can take out several passengers.

Chumming—Scattering small bits of food into the water to attract and hold fish in an area where they can be caught.

Cone—A cover on spincasting reels that prevents the line from coming off the spool during the cast. It also protects the spool from dirt and grit. It is also called a "nose cone," or "reel cover."

Conservation—The wise use of natural resources.

Cove—A small bay or inlet in a body of water.

Crankbait—A term for what is commonly called a plug. Usually these are plastic lures designed to dive under the water's surface.

Creel—A fish basket or personal fish carrier used to carry fish when fishing on or near shore.

Creel Limit—A term used by some fisheries agencies to tell the number of fish by species that can be legally caught in one day.

Current—Any movement of water, whether caused by tides, ocean water movements, or flowing water, in rivers and streams.

Depth Finder—Also called fish finder or sonar, they are devices that signal the bottom and record it on a flashing dial, LCD screen, or graph paper.

Detritus—Particles of rock or other material worn away from a mass by action of water; disintegrated material; debris.

Dissolved Oxygen—(DO): The oxygen utilized by fish which is put into water by forces such as wind, plants, microorganisms, etc.

DNR—An abbreviation for the Department of Natural Resources, the agency in many states responsible for fisheries management and conservation.

Dorsal Fin—A fin located on the back or uppermost part of a fish.

Double Taper— A type of fly line that has a thin, long center portion (belly) with tapers at both ends.

Downrigger—A fishing device used on boats that allows fishing very deep with light tackle. It consists of a reel of heavy line or cable, a heavy weight to keep the cable stretched, and release clips into which the fishing line is fastened and then released when a fish hits. This allows the angler to determine the depth to troll the lures.

Drag Anchor—An anchor used for fishing in currents. The anchor is designed to slip, allowing the boat to move with the current. A length of heavy chain is often used.

Drag Knob—The knob that allows the adjustment of the reel's drag pressure.

Drag System—A system in any reel that serves as a braking mechanism to slow a fish as it pulls line off of a reel. Drag pressure is usually set to 1/4 to 1/3 of the line test.

Dry Fly—A fishing fly tied to stiff hackle material which allows it to float and imitate an adult stage of a stream insect such as a may fly, caddis fly, or stone fly.

Ecology—The branch of biology dealing with the relationship of organisms and their environment.

Ecosystem—A complex ecological community and environment forming a functioning whole in nature.

Epilimnion—The warm layer of water above the thermocline.

Erosion—The process by which the surface of the earth is being constantly worn away. The most important elements responsible for erosion are rivers and streams, wind, waves, and glaciers.

Estuary—A water passage where the tide meets a river current; where salt and fresh water meet.

Ethical—Judging behavior, right or wrong, based on a set of values or opinions.

Eutrophic—Lake type used to describe bodies of water characterized by high levels of nutrients in proportion to their total volume of water.

Eye—The part of a fish hook where line is attached or where the hook is attached to a lure.

Fillet—The act of removing the boneless, edible portion of the fish. Filleting involves cutting out the flesh and then (usually) skinning the fish to leave a boneless strip of fish. Also, the portion of the fish cut out and ready to cook.

Fillet Knife—A long-bladed, thin, flexible knife used to fillet fish.

Fingerling—A young fish, about as long as your finger.

Fisheries Management—The effort to use wild populations for human use without destroying them.

Flasher—A type of depth finder that records the depth and bottom structures by blips of light on a circular dial.

Flipping—A method of fishing, usually for largemouth bass, that involves swinging the rod so as to drop the lure or bait into a selected spot.

Float—See bobber.

Float Plan—A plan which should be filed by every boater with someone on shore, that tells the plans for the day.

Flotsam— Floating wreckage of a ship or its cargo; any miscellaneous material floating in the water.

Fly—An artificial lure tied on a hook and made of fur, feathers, tinsel, wool, synthetic dubbing, thread, etc., and designed to be cast with a fly fishing outfit.

Fly Tying—The craft of tying flies, i.e., wrapping thread around fly tying hooks to secure the materials to imitate insects, bugs, and aquatic insects.

Food Chain—Chain of organisms in any natural community. Each link in the chain feeds on and obtains energy from the one before it and, in turn, is eaten by and provides energy for the next. The food chains in a community make up the food cycle or food web.

Fresh Water— Water that contains little or no salt.

Fry—A method of cooking fish in hot oil; Small young fish that have just hatched out of the egg and up to several inches long, at which point they are called fingerlings.

Gaff—A "j" shaped, barbless hook on a long handle used to hook large fish to help with landing.

Gig—Like a harpoon but with several barbed points and used to capture small fish.

Gill—An arch-like breathing organ located behind the gill cover on a fish's head.

Gill Net—A commercial net that has a mesh size designed to catch fish by the gills, preventing them from backing away and escaping. Different mesh sizes are used for different fish species and sizes.

Gorge—A primitive type of hook consisting of a sharpened short stick or bone, tied in the center and holding bait. When eaten by a fish, a gorge becomes lodged in the fish's throat or gullet.

Gradient—The rate at which a road, river channel, or stream, etc., rises or falls.

Graph Recorder—Depth finder that records all information on a roll of graph paper.

Grip—That part of the rod which is held by the angler. Usually made of cork or synthetic material.

Guides—Circular rings made of metal or synthetic materials (aluminum oxide, silicone carbide, etc.) attached to the rod blank and through which the line travels.

Habitat—The type of place where a species of fish lives.

Hackle—Filaments of a cock feather projecting downward from the head of an artificial fly.

Hackle Pliers—Special spring operated pliers designed to hold hackle when tying flies, to enable wrapping the hackle around the hook shank.

Handle—The part of the reel which is held and turned to retrieve line.

Harpoon—A pointed, barbed spear used for spearing and capturing fish.

Herbivore—A plant eating mammal.

Hip Boots—Rubber or synthetic waterproof boots that come up to the hips (crotch) and are used by wading anglers.

Hook Keeper—A small device, usually made of wire, to hold a lure or hook when the rod is not being used.

Hull—The portion of a boat which is in contact with the water.

Hypothermia—Rapid and abnormal chilling of the body to the point where it cannot regain warmth under existing conditions. Thought of as a condition that occurs only in cold weather, it can also occur in mild and even warm weather. Victims must be warmed by special means to prevent greater or long-term damage or death.

I.G.F.A.—Abbreviation for the International Game Fish Association, an organization devoted to keeping records on fish catches and for supporting sportfishing ventures.

Ice Auger—A large ice drill used to cut a hole in the ice for fishing.

Ice Spud—A long heavy chisel-like device used to cut a hole in ice for fishing.

Ichthyology—The branch of zoology that deals with fish, their classification, structure, habits, and life history.

Impoundment—A natural or artificial place where water is collected and stored for use. See Reservoir.

Jig—Lead molded onto a special jig hook. Tail material of rubber, feathers or fur and various combinations of these may be tied onto the hook shank.

Jigging—Fishing using an up-and-down motion with the rod.

Johnboat—A small, usually aluminum, square-bow boat designed for quiet water or river fishing; ranges in length from 10–16 feet.

Lake Classifications—Broad categories of lake types; oligotrophic (infertile), mesotrophic (fertile), eutrophic (very fertile).

Lateral Line System—System of sense organs present in aquatic vertebrates (fish) in pores or canals arranged in a line down the length of each side of the body. It detects pressure changes, including vibrations (low frequency sounds) in water.

LCD Recorder—Abbreviation for **L**iquid-**C**rystal **D**isplay. Depth finder or sonar which records the information on an LCD screen, much like the material used in digital watch faces.

Leader—Any material used between the main line and the lure or hook. Can be monofilament, single stand wire, braided wire or cable. Can be lighter or heavier than the main fishing line. Often used for toothy fish to prevent them from breaking or cutting off.

Levelwind—The part of a bait-casting reel that ensures the line is rewound evenly onto the spool.

Livewell—An aerated container, built into a boat for storing fish and keeping them alive.

Lob Cast—A slow cast used when fishing so as not to throw bait off the hook during the cast.

Lure—Name for any artificial bait used to attract fish.

Map—A drawing of features on land maps are useful in finding streams and access to rivers and lakes. See "chart." Topographical maps are useful since they show contour elevations and various natural features under the water.

Marl—A type of bottom under a body of water which is a mixture of clay and carbonate of lime.

Migration—The movement of animals, including fish, from one area to another.

Monofilament Line—A single, strong synthetic fiber used for fishing line.

Natural Bait—Bait that is organic and common to fish's habitat.

Net—A mesh woven material used to capture fish. Large nets are used for commercial fishing and small nets by anglers to land fish caught on sporting tackle.

Neuston—Minute organisms that float in the surface film of water.

Non-point-source pollution—Pollution that enters water through run-off from land.

Nose Cone—See CONE.

Nymph—Larval phase of an aquatic insect. Also, a fly tied to imitate a nymph, used primarily when trout fishing.

Olfactory Nerves—Nerves that allow for the sense of smell.

Oligotrophic—Lake type used to describe bodies of water characterized by low amounts of nutrients in proportion to their total volume of water.

Open-face—A Spinning reel that has the spool uncovered or exposed.

Organism—Any living thing.

Outrigger—A long pole that extends from the side of a fishing boat and used with lines and release clips to allow greater variety in trolling.

Oxygen—Necessary for all life, including fish life. Found dissolved in water and taken in by fish through the gills.

Panfish—A small fish such as a bluegill, sunfish, or crappie which fits into a frypan.

Pectoral Fin—Either of the fins of a fish that corresponds to the forelimbs of a four-legged animal.

Pelvic Fin—One of the paired fins of a fish, comparable to the hind limbs of a four-legged animal.

PFD—An abbreviation for Personal Flotation Device, the technical term for a life vest.

pH—The hydrogen ion content, or the acidity or alkalinity of any substance. In water, most fish find neutral pH most comfortable based on a scale of 0 to 14, neutral being in the middle. A low pH means acidic water while high pH is caustic or alkaline. Either condition, in the extreme, can harm fish.

Photosnythesis—The process by which plant cells make carbohydrates from water and carbon dioxide in the presence of chlorophyll and sunlight.

Planer—A device that will cause fishing line to angle down and take a lure far deeper than it would normally run.

Population Density—The number of individuals of a given population occupying a unit of space. For example, the number of bass per acre.

Practice Plug—A special no-hook hard rubber or plastic weight used to practice casting.

Predator—A fish that feeds on other fish.

Predator-Prey—An interdependence between a species and an accessible forage.

Pumping—A method of fighting fish that involves raising the rod to pull the fish closer, then gaining line by reeling as the rod is lowered.

Push Button—A lever or knob on a spincast reel. Pressing the push button holds the line in place until pressure is released, at which time the line and lure can be cast.

Quarry—Prey; anything hunted.

Reading Water—The ability to look at a body of water and to select the most likely spots which would hold fish.

Redd—Nest dug for spawning.

Reel Body—The part of the reel that holds the gears and other controls.

Reel Foot—Reel part used to hold the reel on the rod. It is held by the reel seat.

Reel Seat—That part of a rod designed to grip a reel by the reel foot.

Reservoir—Impoundment. A lake where water is collected and stored for use, usually behind a dam.

Retrieve—The act of rewinding line onto a reel spool and retrieving a bait or lure.

Rigging—The process of attaching a lure or bait for a particular situation or species of fish.

Rod Butt—The end of the rod handle.

Salt Water—Water with salt in it, such as the ocean or the sea.

Sand Spike—A pointed hollow tube, usually of aluminum or plastic, designed to stick upright in sand to hold a surf rod.

Scale—1. A chitinous covering plate on a fish. 2. A method (scaling) of removing the scales from a fish for cooking and eating. 3. A gauge used to weigh fish.

School (of fish)—A number of fish of a species that are grouped together for mutual advantage.

Scoring—A method of preparing fish by making narrow cuts almost all the way through, which allows hot oil to cook up the small bones.

Season—The period of time during a year that a particular species of fish may be harvested.

Sediment—The matter that settles to the bottom of a liquid such as water.

Sedimentation—The accumulation of sediment.

Sensor—A device that responds to a physical stimulus (such as heat, light, or motion) and transmits an impulse.

Setting the Hook—The process of embedding a hook in a fish's mouth.

Shank—The longest part of most fish hooks, between the eye and the bend of the hook.

Side Planer—A planer which runs to the side of the boat for trolling.

Sinker—A weight used to get a lure or bait down deeper into the water.

Skirted Spool—A type of spool found on open face spinning reels where a flange extends from the rear of the spool to cover the cup and spool housing.

Slough—A swampy place; marshy inlet.

Snagging—Casting a heavy sinker and large treble hook with no bait. The angler tries to hook the body of a fish by making strong pulls on the rod.

Snag—An underwater structure that tends to cause a lure or bait to become hung up.

Snap Swivel—Like a snap, but with the addition of a swivel to help prevent line twist.

Snelled Hook—A hook that is pre-tied with a short length leader.

Sonar—Same as depth finder.

Spaghetti Tag—A long, thin tag, resembling spaghetti, used to mark fish for migration and other studies.

Spawning Run—The movement of fish to a location for spawning.

Species—A biological classification of plants and animals.

Spincast Lures—Lures of all types that are fished with spincast tackle.

Spinner—A standard lure that consists of a rotating blade on a shaft that holds a body or beads and ends with a hook.

Spinnerbait—A lure consisting of a weighted head and hook (like a jig) molded onto a right angle safety pin wire that holds a blade or blades. There are single and double-blade styles.

Spinning Lures—Lures of all types that are fished with spinning tackle.

Spool—Device to hold the line on any reel.

Spoon—A lure made of metal and designed to imitate a baitfish. Includes jigging spoons for fishing vertically; trolling spoons; and weedless spoons with weed guards.

Sport Fishing—Fishing for recreation and not for profit or commercial reasons.

Star Drag—A drag system consisting of several layers of soft and hard washers in a reel and controlled by a star-shaped wheel.

Steak—A chunk of fish that is made by cutting fish into steaks by transverse cuts through the body. Used for larger fish.

Stern—The rear end of a boat.

Stickbait—A floating plug or artificial lure of wood or plastic that has no action and must be manipulated by the angler.

Still Fishing—A method of fishing where the bait is cast to a spot and the angler waits for the fish to bite.

Streamer—A type of fly tied to a long shank hook, using feathers for the "wing" and designed to imitate a stream minnow.

Strike—The point at which a fish hits or engulfs a lure. Also a known as "to strike" a fish; to set the hook.

Strike Drag—A heavier than normal drag often set to strike a fish and drive the hook in the fish. Most often used with the drag system on offshore reels.

Structure—A term used by anglers to designate any type of object or cover attractive to fish. Structure that fish relate to includes stumps, rock piles, log jams, piers, docks, boat houses, reefs, artificial reefs, channel markers, points of land, weed lines, etc.

Subsistence Fishing—Fishing for food rather than for sport.

Suspended Fish—Fish which are hovering considerably above the bottom in open water.

Swivel—A small fastener consisting of two eyes with a central barrel or swiveling portion. Designed for fastening lines and line/leader combinations to help prevent line twist through lure action.

Tack—A slanting or zig-zag course against the wind or waves.

Tackle—A name given to fishing equipment or gear.

Tackle Balance—A term used to describe how a rod, reel, line, and lure should be matched. Reel size, rod stiffness, line strength, lure weight, and fish size must all be matched to proper casting and fish fighting.

Tackle Box—A portable storage unit used to organize and transport fishing tackle.

Tailer—A fish landing device that works like a noose to snare fish by the tail.

Tapered Leader—A leader used in fly fishing. Thick at one end, it tapers to a thinner end, or tippet, the end where the fly is tied.

Taxidermy—A method by which fish are preserved for mounting as a trophy.

Terminal Tackle—The hooks, weights, swivels, and other fishing tackle attached on or near the end of your fishing line.

Test—Line strength as stated on the label.

Thermocline—Temperature stratification in a body of water. The layer of water where temperature changes at least one half a degree per foot of depth.

Tight-Line Fishing—A method of fishing with live or natural bait where the angler lets the sinker take the bait down, then tightens the line when the bait is on the bottom. Used without a bobber or float.

Tippet—The small, front section of a tapered leader to which the lure is attached.

Tournament—A fishing contest with prize categories based on weight of fish or total catch. Many tournaments today are release tournaments in which the fish are released after being weighed.

Tourniquet—A device for stopping bleeding by compressing a blood vessel by using a bandage tightened by twisting with a stick

Transom—The rear of the boat; the portion onto which the motor is mounted.

Treble—A hook with three points used on many lures and for bait fishing.

Trolling—A method by which lures or bait are trailed on the end of fishing line, behind or to the side of a moving boat. This makes it possible to fish a large area rapidly.

Turbid—Not clear; muddy; cloudy.

Turnover Period—A very brief period when a lake is in turmoil. A mixing or "turning over" of the water takes place as cold water on the surface settles and water from below rises. This turnover homogenizes lakes that have stratified (layered according to water temperature) in summer and reoxygenates the water.

Ultralight—A name given to casting equipment that is reduced in size for casting small, lightweight lures.

Viscosity—The resistance of a fluid to the motion of its molecules among themselves; thickness; stickiness.

Waders—Long rubberized or synthetic boots that extend up to the mid-chest or armpit area for wading in deep waters while fishing. Allow for deeper wading than hip boots.

Water Pollution—The contamination of water. Water pollution often limits the amount of fish in a body of water or eliminates them entirely.

Watershed—The region drained by one river system.

Weedless—A hook or lure that tends to pass through aquatic vegetation without picking any up.

Weight Forward Taper—A fly line with the heavy thick "belly" portion towards the front, with a front taper leading to the end to attach the leader, and a rear taper leading to a long line that is thin and takes little room on the reel.

Weir—A channel or fencing of stones or sticks placed in the water to guide fish into an area where they can be captured.

Wet Fly—A fly that imitates an aquatic or land insect and sinks in the water. Most are made of soft water absorbent materials.

Wrapping—Thread or other material wound around the rod and guide to secure the guide to the rod.